D1135393

# Tips for Better Baking

# Tips for Better Baking

## LUCY YOUNG

EBURY
PRESS

1 3 5 7 9 10 8 6 4 2

Published in 2009 by Ebury Press, an imprint of Ebury Publishing

A Random House Group Company

The Random House Group Limited Reg. No. 954009

Addresses for companies within the Random House Group can be found at
www.randomhouse.co.uk

A CIP catalogue record for this book is available from the British Library

**Mixed Sources**
Product group from well-managed
forests and other controlled sources
www.fsc.org Cert no. TT-COC-2139
© 1996 Forest Stewardship Council

The Random House Group Limited supports The Forest Stewardship
Council (FSC), the leading international forest certification organisation. All our titles that are
printed on Greenpeace approved FSC certified paper carry the FSC logo. Our paper
procurement policy can be found at www.rbooks.co.uk/environment

To buy books by your favourite authors and register for offers visit www.rbooks.co.uk

Printed and bound in the UK by CPI Mackays, Chatham ME5 8TD

ISBN 9780091932343

# CONTENTS

Introduction 7

1 Why bake? 9

2 Baking jargon 13

3 Getting started 17

4 A–Z of equipment & extras 25

5 Essential ingredients 37

6 Easy cakes for everyday 53

7 Small cakes & cookies 69

8 Classic cakes 87

9 Healthy cakes 109

10 Kids' cakes 129

11 Ask Lucy 141

Cooking times & conversion charts 150

Specialist equipment & suppliers 152

# introduction

Food is all about pleasing people, and there is no better way of doing this than with a lovely slice of home-made cake! Many of us are starting to bake more at home; with children, especially, it is a joy to do. From an early age, I used to bake with my mother – from licking the bowl to icing and presenting the masterpiece to the family – it was always a pleasure. In our house, icing and decorating the Christmas cake marked the start of Christmas, and we all had a go; it was a big tradition that my mother still continues with her grandchildren.

Baking is a science, but that doesn't mean that it has to be scary. The basic rule is follow the recipe; otherwise, learn from my own experience with these better baking tips – with information on ingredients, basic equipment and essential extras, answers to common baking problems via the questions I am most frequently asked, plus specific guidance to all our most popular cakes, cookies and biscuits and how best to make them with success. You'll find everything you need here for foolproof baking, so you can turn out a perfect cake, each and every time. Good luck and enjoy!

## Five golden rules

- preheat the oven to the correct temperature

- weigh the ingredients accurately

- use the right size tin

- put in the right place in the oven

- bake for the specified time

# why bake?

If you've never baked a cake or feel that you are too busy to do so, why not think again. Baking is one of life's simpler pleasures, in so many ways.

# 5 reasons to bake

## Economy

You're in charge, so you can choose the best ingredients you can afford; you can make home baking more economical than shop bought. And treat yourself to more expensive, quality ingredients for special occasions. Plus home-made cakes have none of the shop-bought packaging or baggage that is so burdensome for the environment.

## Enjoyment

In the time it takes to get to the shops and buy a cake, you could have one baking in the oven – and spend an enjoyable half hour. Plus you'll enjoy the extra kick you get from serving it, knowing that you made it yourself.

## Family fun

It's great to learn new things yourself and to teach the kids some new skills too – all you need is a large mixing bowl and a wooden spoon to make the most basic cakes, such as flapjacks (p.67). And even avoid the oven altogether, if you prefer, and make a plate of fridge cakes (p.131).

# Health

Knowing what's in your food is a comfort. Trying to find your way through the labelling of shop-bought cakes is hard; apart from the additives, the cakes are often not baked-on-the-day fresh. But when you bake a cake yourself, you can eat it the day it's made – or freeze it – and it's up to you what goes in it.

You can reduce or leave out salt altogether, if you want (though some people think a pinch of salt can do a lot for flavour, I believe cakes don't need added salt, so all my cake recipes are largely salt free); go organic, if you prefer; choose recipes with a low sugar content, such as my dairy-free fruit loaf (p.120), for example, which uses fruit for sweetness, and has no eggs (like flapjacks, too, p.67); include wholemeal flour when it's an option (p.50); substitute light soft cheese, skimmed milk and half-fat crème fraîche, if appropriate; make no fat cakes (p.118), if required; add lots of fruit and fibre, a few seeds and nuts for health (pp.123 and 115); build up to your 5-a-day with veg, such as courgettes and carrots (p.114).

You can also be confident of the absence of foods that are no-go in your household, such as nuts, for those with nut allergies; cater for special diets, such as low cholesterol (for which whisked sponges are good as they have no fat, see p.60).

*why bake?*

## Taste

East, west, home's best! Not only do you get those wonderful baking aromas that make a house a home, but you can also pick and adapt your own recipe to suit your taste (don't like ginger? so leave it out) and choose the quality of the ingredients (the best butter has the best flavour).

How can you resist?

# baking jargon

# the language of baking

A number of people have mentioned that they would enjoy baking – if they could understand it! With this in mind, here's my selection of some baffling baking basics.

***Bain-marie*** French word to describe a method of cooking in a pan or tin half-filled with hot water. Ensures gentle cooking therefore common with egg bakes, e.g. crème caramel.

***Bake blind*** To bake an unfilled raw flan or pie pastry case until golden and cooked then fill with cold filling or flavourings and bake again.

**How to bake blind** *Line the greased tin with the raw pastry, then prick the pastry all over with a fork. This ensures the pastry stays flat on the base of the tin and does not rise. Cover the pricked pastry with a sheet of baking parchment or greaseproof paper and fill with baking beans or rice so that the pastry stays flat and cooks evenly*

*Blend* Mix together two or more ingredients with a spoon, fork or blender until smooth.

*Cream (or Beat)* Mix together two or more ingredients with a wooden spoon, usually butter and sugar, until they are smooth and fluffy. The light texture of sponge cakes, such as traybakes, comes partly from creaming the sugar and fat.

*Crimp* To pinch or press pastry edges to seal a pie or tart and make an attractive scallop-pattern edge.

*Cut and fold (or just Fold)* A gentle technique for combining light, airy mixtures, e.g. whisked egg whites, with a slightly heavier mixture, such as flour, without stirring and causing loss of air. Use a sharp-sided spoon and cut through the middle of the mixture, run along the side and fold the mixture over the top. Repeat gently until ingredients are evenly combined.

*Drizzle* Carefully pour or trickle a liquid or icing in a fine stream to give a light coating.

*Egg wash* A whole egg, egg white or yolk mixed with a small amount of water or milk and used as a glaze that is brushed over raw pastry and breads to give a golden glaze when baked.

*Grease (or Butter)* Cover the base and sides of a cake tin with a smear of butter or lard to prevent the cake from sticking.

*Line* Lining a tin with non-stick baking parchment makes it easier to remove the cake from the tin after baking and cooling.

*Whip* See *whisk* Often used with reference to cream.

*Whisk* To incorporate air for extra volume for a lighter mix – usually for cream or eggs. Can use a hand-held manual whisk, for gentle whisking, or an electric whisk, e.g. for meringues or whipping cream.

*Whiz* The action of using a food processor or blender to combine ingredients or chop or make them smooth.

*See also* Equipment, pp.24–36, for more on cake tins and baking papers, electric mixers and food processors etc; Ingredients, pp.37–52; Ask Lucy, pp.141–47.

# getting started

Baking ground rules

A word about cake tins

Getting the best from your oven

Some Aga notes

Storage & freezing checklist

Cake baking is as much a science as an art; with this in mind, here are the essential pointers to success.

# The ground rules

Get organised – before you start read through the recipe to make sure you have everything you need, including non-food items such as tins

- Follow the recipe accurately

- Measure out your ingredients carefully

- Weigh in imperial or metric – don't be tempted to mix the two

- Take care not to over beat the cake mix if you want your cake to rise

- Don't beat or stir a mix too roughly when folding in – and use a sharp-edged spoon – or you risk knocking out the essential air

- Bake a cake as soon as it's mixed – don't leave it sitting around or it will lose the added air (except fruit cakes, see p.90)

- Use the correct baking time – don't over bake or your cake will burn or end up dry, but do be aware that all ovens and Agas are different

- Generally, the centre of the oven is best for baking; for Agas, see p.21

- Invest in a wire cooling rack to set the cake tin on after baking for vital air circulation to avoid a soggy base

# Cake tins

- Size matters – use the right tin for the recipe; using a smaller or a larger one, a round tin instead of a square one will alter the cooking time. Even a small difference makes a difference

- Do grease and line your tins as this helps stop cakes sticking and burning

- I always use butter or soft margarine (not oil) to grease a tin, because it is better for flavour

- If cake sticks to the sides, run a small palette knife around the edges or try greasing it more thoroughly next time

- Cleaning is easy if you line your tins with a reusable non-stick silicone liner, such as Bake-O-Glide or Lift-Off paper

- Don't be tempted to over-fill – halfway up is about right

*getting started*

## How to line a cake tin

You can buy pre-cut discs and liners from specialist cook shops; otherwise it's easy to cut out your own.

*To base line* Put the tin on a sheet of non-stick baking parchment and draw around the base with a pencil. Remove the tin and cut out the circle or rectangle marked in pencil, which should fit snugly into the bottom of the tin (remember to grease first).

*To side line* Cut out a length of baking parchment slightly longer (to allow for an overlap) than the tin's circumference. Fold the paper in half lengthways and cut along the fold. You will have two lengths suitable for lining the sides, so put the other one away until you need it.

*An easy way to foil line a rectangular tin, like a roasting tin or traybake* Turn the tin upside down, mould the foil over the top, turn the tin back over; the foil case will drop neatly into the tin.

# Ovens

All ovens – gas, electric or Aga – have their funny ways, but some general guidelines are worth considering.

- Preheat oven to temperature so your cake goes in at the right heat

- Most ovens have hotspots, so get to know yours – you may need to turn the tin around halfway through for even baking; or bake for slightly less or more time as some ovens cook quicker or slower than others

- The centre of the oven, where the air is able to circulate fully around the cake, is generally best for cake baking

- Don't open the door too early at the start – wait until at least halfway through cooking time before you first take a peep

- Always close oven doors gently, without creating a swish of air by slamming

- If your cake rises unevenly, it could be that you didn't preheat the oven to temperature before baking or that it was baked on an uneven shelf

- If baking more than one tin at once, expect it to take a little longer and swap shelves halfway through

## Oven temperature

You can get a rough idea of whether your oven is set at the right temperature by looking at your cakes:

- If the top of your sponge cake is evenly golden and gently rounded or flat, your oven temperature is correct

- If a cake has a peak and cooks faster than the recipe suggests, your oven is too hot

- If a cake sinks a little, takes longer to bake than suggested in the recipe and has a rough texture, your oven is too cool

- To be sure, why not invest in an oven thermometer

## A special oven: the Aga

As Agas are a passion and specialism of mine, I am including a few Aga-baking guidelines to supplement the Aga-cooking instructions given in the recipe sections. For more detailed Aga-baking ideas, see my book *Secrets of Aga Cakes* (Ebury, 2007).

- 2-oven Agas: bake on the grid shelf on the floor of the roasting oven with the cold sheet on the second set of runners above – this lowers the temperature of the oven, preventing the cake from burning

- 3- and 4-oven Agas: bake on the grid shelf on the floor of the baking oven, with the option of using the cold sheet if the cake is getting too brown

- In 2-oven Agas, very deep cakes need to be baked in an Aga cake baker

- Rich deep fruit cakes are baked in the simmering oven with great success

- Drop scones and pancakes do not need a griddle pan, they can be cooked directly on the simmering plate

- If making a whisked sponge, warm the sugar in the simmering or warming oven to give more bulk when whisking

- Use the back and sides of the Aga for melting e.g. chocolate or butter

- To make jam easier to spread, warm in the jar on the back of the Aga or in the simmering oven for about 10 mins

- If squeezing juice from citrus fruit, warm the whole fruit in the simmering oven for about 15 mins before squeezing and you will get more juice from the fruit

# Storage and freezing checklist

Once baked, your cake needs a little after-care.

- Store in a cake tin in a cool, dry place – otherwise, in a warm kitchen, for example, or near heat, they can quickly turn mouldy

- Store cakes and biscuits separately as the moisture from the cakes will make the biscuits go soggy

- Small cakes dry out faster than large ones, so consider freezing any left over on the day for another occasion

- If iced with cream or other dairy products, keep the cake in the fridge covered with cling film

- Most cakes freeze well un-iced or iced – it's preferable, though, to freeze un-iced and ice on the day so that the icing looks shiny and fresh

- Freeze a cold cake wrapped in cling film in a sealed plastic bag

- Freeze cakes flat and don't sit anything on top of them

# a–z
## of equipment
## & extras

**Baking equipment essentials**

**Baking kit extras**

You don't need a stash of specialist baking equipment – you can make many cakes by hand with excellent results, though most cakes are easier with an electric mixer. You've probably got many of the essentials already; the optional extras are good to have at some point.

# essentials: a–z

**Baking Sheet** Heavyweight and flat baking tin, with slight lip around the edge, preferably a good-quality solid one that conducts heat well and doesn't buckle in the oven. Make sure you buy a size that fits your oven (though not too tight a fit). Having two is ideal, especially if you are a keen biscuit baker, as biscuits spread during baking and take up a lot of room (two trays are required for one recipe); also perfect for scones and gingerbread men.

**Baking Tins** You can buy tins in a range of sizes and materials, including lightweight aluminium, hard anodized aluminium, stainless steel; some are silicon coated to make them a lightweight non-stick.

*I find the modern non-stick tins very good but still base line with non-stick baking paper to make cakes easier to remove from the tin*

Tins with a reinforced rolled rim are especially sturdy – the rim stops the tins buckling or changing shape in a hot oven – and look out for securely welded corners. A good, solid base keeps the cake flat and prevents buckling. I am not so keen on tins with a padded, raised base, as the bottom of the cake takes longer to cook. For convenience, check that tins are dishwasher, fridge and freezer safe.

*Matt, dark-coloured tins absorb more heat than shiny, light-coloured ones, and will therefore cook cakes a little faster*

*Sandwich cake tin* Named after the Victoria Sandwich Cake (see p.000 for the recipe) – round, usually with a loose bottom that can be pushed up so that the cake is easy to remove. *Springform tin* Round or square and deeper than a sandwich tin; the springform clip at the sides releases to make it easier to get the cake out of the tin. Perfect for deep cakes and cheesecakes. *Traybake tin* Like a small roasting tin but named after the easiest of all cakes, the traybake, a good size is 30 x 23 x 4 cm (9 x 12 x 1 ½ in). *Swiss roll tin* Similar to a traybake tin but very shallow, about 2 cm (1 in) deep.

> *Buy the best-quality cakes tins you can afford – they will
> not only last a lifetime but also guarantee an even spread
> of heat for successful baking*

Other basic tins include a *loaf tin*; 500 g (1 lb) is a useful size. *Bun tins* are shallower and more angled than *muffin tins* and perfect for fairy cakes.

**Baking Parchment** A shiny, non-stick silicone paper, suitable for baking, in particular to stop cakes from sticking to the tin and help avoid over-cooking; *greaseproof paper* is matt and not non-stick, and increasingly being replaced by baking parchment. Some non-stick graphite papers can be wiped clean and re-used and are therefore a worthwhile investment.

> *I still line non-stick tins with a disc of parchment as it
> makes it easier to remove it from the tin*

**Electric Kitchen Tools** A great help in the kitchen for ease and to speed up mixing. *An electric hand mixer* is mobile, easy to clean and perfect for quickly whisking egg whites and cake mixtures; though beware of over-beating. If you have a large batch of egg whites, say for meringues, it will still take a long time to whisk because the smaller the whisk the longer the whisking.

A *free-standing/table-top electric mixer* is a powerful machine with a large bowl and whisk or hook (not a machine with a metal blade – this is a *food processor*). It is good for effortless mixing and whisking of cake mixtures. I'd recommend KitchenAid or Kenwood mixers: simple and fast to use, they have a large bowl and large whisk for mixing and whisking.

A *free-standing food processor* is a powerful machine with a large bowl, metal or plastic blade and lid for food preparation – for chopping, mixing, blending but not whisking – that also has attachments for grating and slicing.

*If you use an electric mixer, don't over whisk or you risk beating out all the air and finishing up with a flat cake*

**Foil** I find greased kitchen foil useful to line traybake tins – you can easily remove the traybake from the tin, as the foil is sturdier than paper, and if you ice the cake in the foil, it holds its shape. Which is the right or wrong side of foil to use? I find it makes no difference!

**Hand-held/Manual Whisk** A stainless-steel hand-held wire balloon whisk is useful for blending and whisking, though not when you need to get a lot of air into something as it takes too long; this is best done with an electric whisk. Look out for one with a handle that you find easy to use – vital for lengthy whisking sessions.

**Knives** Flat-bladed *palette knives* – two sizes are useful, one large and a flexible small one for running around the edge of a cooked cake in the tin or for spreading icing. A small *serrated knife* for cutting fruit and a serrated *bread knife* for trimming cakes, e.g. Swiss rolls.

**Measuring Jug** For measuring liquids – traditional glass or lightweight plastic, whichever you prefer.

*When measuring on a table top, bend down so you are at eye level and you can see the exact measurement – if you look standing up you could be out by as much as 20 ml*

**Measuring Scales** Your best bet is a good pair of *balance scales* – not cheap but a lifetime's investment. *Digital scales* Some people like them, but I find that they can be temperamental, especially when the battery is running low; if you buy digital scales with a plug in cord then these are fine and will be accurate. Needle-indicator type not 100 per cent reliable as the spring can lose its bounce and breaks easily.

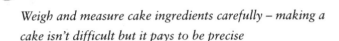

*Weigh and measure cake ingredients carefully – making a cake isn't difficult but it pays to be precise*

**Measuring Spoons** such as a heavy-duty plastic or stainless-steel set are invaluably accurate.

**Mixing Bowls** You can get by with whatever bowls you have, but a big mixing bowl ensures that you get air into the mix – good to ensure cakes rise. Traditional ceramic or glass stacking bowls, such as Pyrex, come in various sizes; plastic and stainless steel are good too, whichever appeals to you.

**Pastry Brush** For glazing with egg, oil or milk. Either natural bristle or plastic – either is good, but I prefer the flat bristles (like a paint brush) rather than the rounded ones.

**Rolling Pin** For rolling out pastry, bashing biscuit crumbs and icing – a useful size is about 40 cm (15 in) with flat ends and no handles. The ceramic ones are good for pastry as they stay cool and stop the pastry from sweating. I use a wooden one!

**Sieves/Strainers** A round metal or nylon (with plastic, heat-resistant handles) *sieve/strainer* for sifting in flour, cocoa powder, icing sugar and sieving fruit. One large and one small is ideal; they are often available in sets of three in different sizes. I prefer *nylon sieves* as these can be used for anything; the metal sieves are not ideal for sieving acidic fruit, for example, as the metal can taint the flavour.

*Sifting in flour with a sieve is a gentle way of adding flour to already whisked mixtures*

**Spatulas & Spoons** A flexible *plastic/silicone spatula* – for scraping the last of the cake mix from the bowl. A *wooden spoon/spatula* for mixing or stirring (a set in different sizes is useful); a *metal spoon* (a tablespoon is fine) for folding in flour and other dry ingredients.

**Storage Tins** must be airtight with well-fitting lids. You can buy nests of them, in a handy range of sizes, which store easily when not in use – either plastic or metal is good.

**Wire Cooling Rack** Round, square or oblong wire tray, usually chrome-plated or non-stick, with gaps for air to circulate – for sitting hot cakes on to cool down without going soggy. Once cooled, cakes are easier to handle and won't break or crumble so readily. I suggest a rectangular one about 38 x 30 cm (15 x 12 in), if you are keen on making traybakes; a round 25 cm (10 in) cooling rack, if you are keen on round cakes. You can even buy 3-tier ones for big baking days.

# extras: a–z

## For cakes

**Cake Tester** Thin metal wires with loops that make a tiny hole in the cake when testing for done-ness, but a metal skewer or wooden toothpick or skewer does the job too. You can also buy reusable heat-sensing cake testers that turn red when the cake is cooked.

**Cake Server** Thin-bladed triangular knife makes for easy slicing and serving.

**Citrus Squeezer** For catching the pips when squeezing citrus fruit.

**Cookie/Pastry Cutter Set** In various shapes and sizes, including double-sided ones, with one plain and one fluted side; excellent for cutting out scones or biscuits.

*No cookie cutter? Use an inverted glass or saucer instead*

**Oven Thermometer** Handy to double-check your oven temperature, given that in-built oven thermometers are not always entirely accurate.

**Paper Cases** For muffins and buns – non-stick papers and colours, from the plain to the fancy, in a range of sizes.

*Sit paper cases in a bun or muffin tin to help the cakes hold their shape during cooking*

**Shaker/Sifter Set** For dusting on toppings, such as icing sugar or cocoa powder.

**Zester/Stripper** For fine zesting of citrus fruit, to use the zest as an ingredient and for decoration

## For icing

There is a whole variety of specialised equipment for icing and decorating – visit a specialised cake shop for a good choice of cutters, moulds and stencils.

**Icing and Food Piping Bags** I regularly use two sizes of piping bag, a large one for whipped cream and buttercream, and a tiny one for intricate icing for letters or pretty shapes. I prefer nylon as it is easy to clean even in the washing machine.

*An easy way to fill a piping bag* Before filling, remember to put the nozzle in the piping bag! Sit the bag with the point downwards in a tall jug, folding the top of the bag over the rim of the jug. Fill the bag using a spatula and then seal the top and squeeze the contents to the bottom to prevent air bubbles. Twist the top tightly.

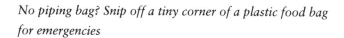

> *No piping bag? Snip off a tiny corner of a plastic food bag for emergencies*

**Nozzles** Available in a range of nozzle sets, but what I find most useful is a plain 1 cm (½ in) one, for piping meringues and biscuits; a rosette nozzle for piping cream and icing. Metal or plastic is fine.

# essential ingredients

Which fats?

Choose your sugar

The role of eggs

Fabulous flours

# the four pillars of cake baking

You don't need to stock up with lots of ingredients – that's one of the joys of baking: at no stage does it have to be complicated or expensive. It is a plus, though, to use the best-quality ingredients you can afford. The best butter, for example, makes a difference to taste and texture; always use butter where flavour is key, such as for shortbread (see p. 104) – the buttery taste is so much part of the enjoyment. Most cakes are a variation on the theme of fat – preferably butter – sugar, egg and flour.

## 1 Fats

It's fat that makes cakes melt in the mouth; in baking that is largely the role of butter, with its high fat content (it's basically churned cream).

*Butter* Essential for flavour and successful baking. If you're concerned about keeping your butter intake low, why not just use butter when it really matters – and it really matters in baking. For texture, too, adding softness, and volume because of how it takes in air when beaten with sugar. Oils and other unsaturated liquid fats are generally not so successful for cakes because they don't hold air well when creamed or beaten with sugar; it's the air bubbles incorporated during creaming/beating that help make light cakes.

*Unsalted butter* with its more delicate flavour is generally preferable to salted butter, because you don't need salt in cake baking and too much salt can overpower the subtle, buttery tastes; many older recipes mention salt, but there is no need to add salt to cakes. If you only have salted butter, however, it's fine to use it.

*Leave out extra salt if baking with salted butter*

*Room temperature* is roughly 18–21°C (65–70°F). If you give butter about an hour out of the fridge before you use it, it will make mixing easier and give a smoother raw mix.

*Softened butter* is at room temperature, which allows it to mix more readily with the sugar and other ingredients, enabling maximum air to be incorporated. Make sure it's soft but not melted or oily (unless melted is specified), because melted doesn't always mix well with other ingredients, such as for a sponge cake.

*essential ingredients*

*Cold butter is good for pastry but generally best avoided for making cakes*

*Store* in the original wrapper to minimize heat and light exposure, which can oxidize butter, making its oils and fats decompose and eventually turn stale and rancid. Keep in the coldest part of the fridge apart from strong-smelling foods as butter readily absorbs other food odours. The salt in salted butter means it lasts longer than unsalted butter. A quick check for freshness is whether the inside of the butter, when sliced, is the same colour as the outside: if it's darker on the outside, it's beginning to turn.

Freeze for up to 6 months or so and defrost in the fridge before use.

**Butter alternatives** There are lots of butter substitutes, so choosing one can be quite confusing. If you don't want to use butter, use an alternative with as high a proportion of fat as possible: block fats, such as Stork, are good.

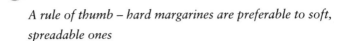

*A rule of thumb – hard margarines are preferable to soft, spreadable ones*

Fats in a tub are often spreads and therefore not good for baking. Spreads generally contain less fat (often no more than 59 per cent fat) and more water than butter, so if you want to use a spread, check its fat content is high enough for baking, even if it says suitable for baking on the tub. Ideally, the proportion of vegetable fat should be over 59 per cent, for example Flora Original, and these are good for cake baking. But do not expect them to taste the same as butter. And they are not necessarily a lower-fat option to butter.

*Never use low-fat spreads for baking – the high water content makes flat cakes*

If using fat in a tub, use it straight from the fridge; otherwise, at room temperature, the fat softens and starts to separate from the water; if you use it like this, your cake will be dense and flat.

*essential ingredients*

## 2 Sugars

Sugar sweetens. It enhances flavour and preserves. It helps bump up the volume too when creamed with butter and improves texture. It's also what turns cakes and biscuits brown. The darker the sugar, the less refined it is; a high molasses content makes for a dark, sticky and strongly flavoured sugar. Most sugar is extracted from sugar cane; the degree of refinement also affects its colour.

*Refined* vs *unrefined sugars* Refined sugars can be white or brown and have been processed to remove the natural molasses and other considered impurities from sugar cane; unrefined sugars are processed as little as possible, just enough to press out, clean and crystallise the sugar cane's natural juice, so the natural molasses and other elements remain to make it more flavoursome and a natural shade of brown colour, ranging from golden through light to dark brown.

*White sugar* vs *brown sugar* White sugar is always refined; not all brown sugars are unrefined: some are minimally processed, that is largely unrefined, and contain natural molasses; others are refined white sugars with an added brown coating for flavour and colour.

*Golden baking sugars* can be used instead of white refined sugars – but, bear in mind, if, for example, you want pure white meringues, they will be a creamy white/brown not white.

*White caster sugar* has very fine crystals that are ideal for baking and produce a fine-textured cake; it avoids a speckled appearance to cakes. Golden caster sugar is the unrefined version. Caster sugar becomes crisp when cooked so excellent for meringues and biscuits.

*White granulated sugar* can be used in some baking, though it tends to give cakes a speckled look and a slightly rougher texture. Golden granulated sugar is the unrefined version.

> *Don't use liquidised granulated sugar for baking – it's too powdery*

*Light brown & dark brown soft sugars* are moist with soft, fine crystals. The light sugar has a 6 per cent or so molasses content, lower than the dark brown sugar, which accounts for its lighter colour and more subtle, fudgy taste. These sugars work well for recipes with a caramel flavour or in toffee or butternut sauce. Because they are soft, they dissolve quickly and don't add texture.

*Dark & light muscovado sugars* are superlative soft brown sugars. Fine grained and moist, dark muscovado has a strong molasses flavour and a rich brown colour that works well in robustly flavoured cakes such as fruit and chocolate cakes and gingerbreads; light muscovado is a warm honey-coloured, fudgy sugar that is especially good for teabreads or treacle cake.

*Muscovado sugar, like all soft brown sugar, tends to harden once opened. To avoid this, soak a piece of kitchen paper in water and lay it on top of the sugar then seal tightly. If you already have hard sugars in your store cupboard, put the sugar in a basin and cover with a damp cloth then leave to soften overnight*

*Demerara sugar* is a raw cane large-crystal sugar with a moist, crunchy texture, 2 per cent molasses content and a rich aroma. Use for baking where crunch counts, such as to give a top texture to biscuits, cookies and cakes, plus the base of a cheesecake.

*Sugar cubes are also useful as a crunchy topping for cakes and biscuits*

*Molasses sugar* has the strongest, richest flavour and darkest, deepest colour of all sugars. It is good for robust fruit and chocolate cakes, for example, but beware its very strong taste doesn't take over. It is not something I often use.

*Icing sugar* is a pulverised white granulated sugar with added anti-caking ingredients that is ideal for icing or dusting cakes. It is unsuitable for cake baking, because it is so fine that it dissolves and adds no texture. Unrefined icing sugar is unprocessed and gives a mellow, natural honey colour and taste; if you ice your Christmas cake with unrefined icing sugar, don't expect it to be snowy white

*essential ingredients*

*Avoid unrefined sugars in recipes such as meringues if you want them to look pure white*

*Vanilla sugar* (usually, more usefully, caster sugar) enhances vanilla flavours in cakes and biscuits – you can make it yourself by splitting a vanilla pod, to release the flavour, and submerging it in a pound/half a kilo or so of caster sugar in a tightly lidded jar for about a week to infuse (and leave it there, because there is no limit on how long it should infuse). It will hold its flavour for a good few months. Keep topping it up as you use it.

*Other sweetening ingredients* include honey, golden syrup, molasses, maple syrup, fruit and sugar-free jams.

*Store* all sugars in a cool, dry place. Sugar is hygroscopic, which means it attracts water; so once opened, keep it in an airtight container to help stop it getting damp or hard.

# 3 Eggs

In baking, eggs are useful to bind together other ingredients; add air to the raw cake mix during beating; as a glaze. Use the specified size – not large when the recipe states medium. Egg is liquid, and the liquid ingredient of recipes is carefully balanced for success. If the egg size is not specified in the ingredients, look for a general note on the recipes, where the preferred egg size is usually given. In this book, eggs are large, unless otherwise stated.

The better-quality egg, the better the cake's texture, colour and flavour. Free-range eggs have brighter yolks and therefore produce a richer colour cake. Try to use organic and free-range for taste and to encourage good farming practice.

*The Lion Quality stamp indicates eggs from hens vaccinated against salmonella – though that doesn't mean they are organic or free-range*

Some people insist that you take eggs out of the fridge for a couple of hours before using them or they can make the cake mix curdle, which can mean you lose more air and end up with a heavier cake. I am rebellious and use them straight from the fridge – even for meringues, I don't notice any difference!

Avoid cracked eggs as the white and yolk are no longer sealed and therefore at risk of infection.

*If using several eggs, break them into a separate bowl, one at a time first, just in case one of them is bad; it will not then ruin the whole cake*

## 4 Flours

There are numerous flour types, but, for baking, the following are most generally used. For best results, always use the flour specified in the recipe.

*Plain white flour* also known as superfine or soft plain flour and 70 per cent wheat grain, from which the bran and wheat germ have been extracted, leaving the white starchy part of the grain. It is the flour most generally used for cooking; in baking, specifically, it is often used with a rising agent, such as baking powder.

*Italian 00 flour* is fine milled and can be used as a plain white flour substitute – it helps make lighter cakes.

*White self-raising flour* mostly used in cakes; essentially plain flour with a handy, standard quantity of rising agent, such as baking powder. It is the rising agent that produces the carbon dioxide during baking that makes the cake expand and creates its light and airy texture. Some cakes require more or less baking powder, in which case the recipe will specify plain flour with a given quantity of baking powder.

*I generally use self-raising flour and baking powder, as I believe this gives the best results*

*Wholemeal self-raising flour* is less refined (more coarse) with 100 per cent of the wheat grain as well as the bran and wheat germ – it is higher in fibre than regular plain flour; a coarser flour with a denser texture, so good for cakes using grated fruit or vegetables, such as carrot or courgette cake. Used for baking, it can result in a slightly drier cake as it absorbs liquids more quickly; so I often add a little milk when using wholemeal flour.

*Use wholemeal and white flours, half and half, so you have some of the benefits of each, but add a little milk to account for the wholemeal flour*

*Wholemeal plain flour* is similar to wholemeal self-raising flour but without the baking powder. For healthy baking, consider wholemeal flour as a possible alternative.

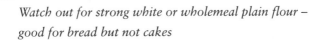

*Watch out for strong white or wholemeal plain flour – good for bread but not cakes*

*Store* flour in a cool, dark, dry place so it doesn't dry out or absorb damp. Keep in an airtight container once open. Flour mites are a threat to old flour, so always use it by the best-before date.

**Baking powder** is a leavening agent that makes cakes rise in the oven (a job also done by the air trapped in the eggs when they are beaten).

Use the right amount of baking powder. Ideally, use a measuring spoon – teaspoon sizes vary too much. Too little baking powder makes for a compact cake; too much, and the cake will collapse as it cools after baking, leaving a telltale central dip – a cake with too much baking powder also tends to fall apart easily.

*Use baking powder by its best-before date – otherwise it won't do its job properly and your cake won't rise well*

# easy cakes for every day

Better Traybakes

Tips on icing

Better Swiss Rolls

Better Sandwich Cakes

Better Flapjacks

A note about food colouring

Tips on filling & dusting

These easy, everyday cakes are confidence builders – fast and foolproof. And, of course, they taste good too. If you're new to baking, this is where I'd suggest you start.

# better traybakes

An all-in-one sponge cake baked, cooled and iced in one tin – no fuss, no mess. Traybakes are ideal for beginners but valued by everyone for their simplicity and adaptability. Perfect for school fêtes, a family tea or, doubled, for a crowd. The basic recipe is economical to make.

- You can make sponge cake mixtures like this by creaming or beating by hand in a large bowl, with a wooden spoon. Or, with an electric hand whisk or free-standing mixer or food processor. But, with electric mixers, especially, don't over-mix or the cake will not rise successfully in the oven

- I use butter, softened, for the best flavour

- Generally, I prefer to use self-raising flour and baking powder as I believe this gives the best results

- Be sure to be accurate when you add milk – always under compensate as you can always add more. Too much milk makes a cake mix too soft and the cake flat

- Sponge or butter cakes like this traybake contain butter, sugar, flour and baking powder, egg and milk in variable amounts, which I combine here via the easy all-in-one method

- When zesting lemons, use unwaxed

- Just leave the cake to cool in the tin and cut into squares, as required – keeps better whole rather than cut

## Iced Lemon Traybake

You won't go wrong with this classic lemon version; always popular at cake stalls. Cuts into 16 pieces. Freezes well un-iced. Store for up to 2 days in an airtight tin.

*for the cake*

225 g (8 oz) soft butter, plus extra for greasing

225 g (8 oz) caster sugar

300 g (10 oz) self-raising flour

2 tsp baking powder

4 eggs

4 tbsp milk

grated zest of 2 lemons, preferably unwaxed

*for the icing*

225 g (8 oz) icing sugar, sifted

about 3 tbsp fresh lemon juice

Preheat oven to 180°C/fan 160°C/gas 4. Foil line and grease a traybake tin (30 x 23 cm/12 x 9 in). Put all the cake ingredients in a bowl and mix together until smooth. Pour into the prepared tin. Bake in the preheated oven for about 30 mins, until golden brown, shrinking from the sides of the tin and springy to touch; in an Aga, on the grid shelf on the floor of the roasting oven with the cold sheet on the second set of runners for about 35 mins. Leave to cool in the tin. To make the icing, sieve the icing sugar over a bowl and mix in the lemon juice. Beat until smooth then spread evenly over the cold cake and leave to set.

# Some icing tips

Sponge cakes, like this traybake, are generally moist, so good un-iced too. But if you have time and decide to ice, there are lots of options. Glacé or water icing keeps cakes fresh, so you can bake and ice ahead – it gives a smooth, flat icing to the cake. If you wish to be creative use a butter icing, though make sure you then store the cake somewhere cool.

## *How best to ice*

- Ice/fill a cold cake or the icing/filling will slide off

- Icing should be a spreading consistency – to coat the top of a cake use a palette knife horizontally (vertically when coating the sides) for a smooth finish

- Spreading icing, especially frosting or any smooth, rich icing, is easier and gives a smoother finish if you dip a palette knife in a jug of hot water, shake to remove any drips then use to spread

- It's always better to ice a cake on the day of eating so the icing keeps its shine and gloss. If freezing cakes, it is best to freeze un-iced and ice on the day of eating

- For cakes that require icing, if you're not going to ice your cake after you've allowed it to cool, wrap it well and ice it as soon as you can

- Covering the top of the cake with jam helps keep the cake moist and prevents the crumbs from the cake from mixing with the icing

- For sugar-topping drizzle icing, drizzle over a warm cake so the juices soak into the sponge – once the cake is cold it won't absorb the juices easily

- Leave heated icings, like fudge icing (p.95), to firm up a little before spreading

## A *word about food colouring & flavouring*

If you want coloured icing, add a drop of food colouring – but make sure it's only a drop, as it can be very strong in colour. I try to avoid it – it's too fake for me. Sometimes with kids' cakes, though, it's not so easy to avoid; so try adding colour with fruit squash (but avoid the light squashes as the colour is not strong enough). Instead of colour, you might like to add a drop of flower water, such as orange blossom water, rose water or lavender, to add a wonderful, natural flavour to icings (but no colour).

# better swiss rolls

A teatime classic, the Swiss roll is a whisked sponge, made without butter, by simply whisking the eggs and sugar, and folding in some flour. Perfect, too, as a light dessert; with no butter, also good for anyone watching their cholesterol.

- For a light cake, get as much air into the egg and sugar mix as possible, so use a large whisk – the eggs and sugar should double in size and be pale in colour

- For extra volume, warm the sugar gently in the microwave or in the simmering or plate-warming oven of an Aga

- Eggs are best used at room temperature for whisked sponges as this makes whisking quicker

- Beware of over-baking – not only dry but also difficult to roll

- Use your favourite jam to fill, when cold – stir chopped fresh fruit into the cream to make it extra special

- Eat fresh – fat helps preserve cakes so fatless sponges don't keep well

- Score before rolling – this will make rolling easier and give a tighter roll

# *Strawberry Swiss Roll*

Cuts into 8 generous slices. Best eaten fresh but store in the fridge for 24 hours. Freezes well filled with cream and jam but not fresh strawberries; once defrosted, serve alongside fresh strawberries.

*for the cake*
4 eggs
100 g (4 oz) caster sugar, plus extra for sprinkling (optional)
100 g (4 oz) self-raising flour
*for the filling*
about 4 tbsp strawberry jam or jam of your choice
300 ml (10 fl oz) double cream, whipped
75 g (3 oz) fresh strawberries, cut into quarters, or fruit of your choice, plus extra to serve (optional)

Preheat oven to 200°C/fan180°C/gas 6. Grease and line a Swiss roll tin 33 x 23 cm (13 x 9 in). Whisk the eggs and sugar, with an electric hand whisk or free-standing electric mixer until they are light, frothy and doubled in size. When the whisk is raised from the mix, it should leave a trail. Sift in the flour in stages, cutting and folding in lightly with a metal spoon. Turn the mixture into a prepared tin, spreading it gently into the corners. Bake in the preheated oven for 10 mins until golden brown and shrinking away from the tin sides; in the Aga on the grid shelf on the floor of the roasting oven for about 8 mins.

While still warm, invert the cake on to a piece of sugared non-stick baking parchment, slightly bigger than the size of the tin. Peel off the lining paper from the cake, trim all the edges and score along one short edge about 2 cm (¾ in) in, without cutting through. While still hot firmly roll up the cake from the scored edge with the baking paper inside. Leave to cool. Once cold, carefully unroll, remove the paper and spread with the jam. Fold the strawberries into the whipped cream and spread the cream over the jam. Re-roll the cake tightly, sprinkle with some caster sugar and keep in the fridge till ready to serve – with fresh fruit alongside, if you wish.

# better sandwich cakes

These traditional English teatime filled sponge cakes are so called because they consist of two (or more) layers, sandwiched together, usually with a filling of whipped cream, buttercream or jam. They look impressive but are not difficult to make.

- Softened butter makes mixing easier

- Using fat helps the cake stay moist

- I find using self-raising flour and baking powder produces the best results

- Divide the mix equally between the two tins so they bake evenly

- Is it cooked? Yes, if it's an even golden brown colour, springy to the touch and shrinks from the tin sides

- To release more easily from the tin, run a palette knife around the outside edge of the cake first

- Variations: add finely grated zest of 2 lemons, oranges or limes into the raw sponge mixture

# Victoria Sandwich Cake

My cake uses only jam as a filling, but you can add whipped cream too if liked. Cuts into 6–8 wedges. Freezes well, plain or filled. Store in an airtight container for up to 2 days.

*for the cake*
225 g (8 oz) butter, softened
225 g (8 oz) caster sugar
225 g (8 oz) self-raising flour
2 level tsp baking powder
4 eggs
*for the filling and dusting*
3 tbsp raspberry jam, to fill
a little caster sugar, to dust

Preheat oven to 180°C/fan 160°C/gas 4. Grease and base line with non-stick baking parchment two 20 cm (8 in) loose-bottomed sandwich tins. Put all cake ingredients into a large bowl and mix together until smooth. Divide the mixture evenly between the prepared tins and level the tops. Bake in the preheated oven for 20–25 mins until well risen, golden brown and coming away from the edges; in an Aga, on the grid shelf on the floor of the roasting oven with the cold sheet on the second set of runners for about 30 mins. Leave to cool in the tins. Turn out and remove the baking parchment. Turn one cake upside down and spread with the jam. Sit the other cake the right way up on top. Sprinkle the top with the caster sugar and serve in slices.

## *Tips for filling & dusting*

- The cake must be cold or the filling will slide out of the cake

- If using jam, warming it a little first makes it easier to spread

- Spreading the middle of a cake with jam helps keeps it moist and stops the crumbs mixing with the icing

- Double cream has a high fat content, which makes it good for fillings or toppings, whipped or piped – but avoid over whipping or you'll end up with butter. Whipping cream is a light, lower-fat alternative

- Dusting with caster sugar rather than icing sugar is traditional and adds a welcome crunch to the softness of the sponge

# better flapjacks

This moist and chewy sweet oatcake with a crisp top is not just easy peasy to do but a healthy, cheap option too – it's basically a traybake that uses oats instead of flour. Kids love them.

- Rolled or porridge oats are best – jumbo oats are too big and don't absorb the other ingredients

- Measure out golden syrup easily by doing so on to the top of another ingredient, such as the sugar, in the weighing pan – the syrup sticks to the sugar, and both ingredients slide easily out of the weighing pan

- Put golden syrup in a warm place to heat a little first to make it easier to pour/spoon from the tin

- Use the right amount of golden syrup – too little, and the flapjack will be dry; too much, and it will be too soft and oily

- I like demerara sugar for its lovely crunch (but soft brown sugar works too)

- Cut flapjack while warm or it will be too hard to slice

- For a variation add 2 teaspoons ground ginger or cinnamon

**Ground spice alert!** *Ground spices, such as ground ginger, have a short shelf life. To use them at their best, buy them in small quantities, store in an airtight container in a dry, cool spot, away from heat, and use by the recommended date*

# Ginger Flapjacks

The ginger adds a welcome edge to the sweetness, but if you are not keen on ginger, just leave it out – it will taste just as good. Cut into 12 wedges. Store in an airtight container for up to 3 days. Suitable for freezing.

100 g (4 oz) butter
100 g (4 oz) demerara sugar
100 g (4 oz) golden syrup
100 g (4 oz) porridge oats
2 tsp ground ginger (optional)
3 stem ginger bulbs, very finely chopped (optional)

Preheat oven to 160°C/fan 140°C/gas 3. Grease and base line 20 cm (8 in) loose-bottomed sandwich tin with a disc of non-stick baking parchment. Gently heat the butter, sugar and golden syrup in a medium pan until the butter has melted and the sugar dissolved. Remove pan from heat and stir in the rolled oats and both gingers. Turn the mixture into the prepared tin and press down firmly with the back of a spoon

*easy cakes for every day*

to level the surface. Bake for about 35 mins in the preheated oven until golden brown; in an Aga, bake on the grid shelf on the floor of the roasting oven with the cold sheet on the second set of runners for about 10–15 mins. Loosen the edges of the flapjacks from the tin sides then leave to cool in the tin for about 10 mins. Invert the flapjacks on to a board and slice into wedges. Leave to cool completely on a wire rack.

# small cakes & cookies

Better Cupcakes & icing/decorating tips

Better Brownies & chocolate tips

Better Muffins

Better Cookies

Small cakes are easy to offer as snacks or include in lunchboxes. Good to share, without the slicing; everyone can have their cake and eat it. There's an element of nostalgia about them too.

# better cupcakes

Cupcakes are cute – and cool; easy to bake and ultra fashionable, the current small cake of choice that started life in America as individual cakes for kids, small enough for tiny hands to hold and easy to take to school in lunchboxes. The classic cupcake is based on our four basic ingredients: butter, sugar, eggs and flour. Any extras, such as chocolate, fruit or flavouring such as vanilla or lavender, are about adding texture and flavour. Most cake recipes can turn into cupcakes – just reduce the cooking time to 15–20 mins and check they're done when they are golden, risen and shrinking away from the cases and an inserted toothpick or skewer emerges clean. They differ from a fairy cake in that they are baked in muffin cases with straight sides as opposed to the angled sides of cake cases used for fairy cakes.

- Use butter for the best flavour

- The combination of self-raising flour and baking powder gives the perfect rise for cupcakes

- Use cupcake tins either greased or lined with a choice of paper, foil or silicone cake cases. You can buy the cases in most supermarkets and kitchen shops, and there are many pretty ones available

- I always line cupcake bun (and muffin) tins with paper cases so the cakes hold their shape in the oven, are easier to remove from the tin and keep moist in their cases

- Make sure your paper cases fit your bun tins neatly – too loose and the cakes could spread out; too tight and they'll wrinkle up

- Each case should be filled leaving a good few cm of a gap at the top to allow for rising and icing

- When dividing the raw mix among the cases, avoid dripping it on to the paper edges, where not only will it look messy and tend to burn but may also prevent the cakes from rising evenly

- Bake on the centre shelf of the pre-heated oven for best heat circulation and turn the tin halfway through to ensure even rising and browning

- Bake until risen and springy – don't overcook or they will be dry

- Cool cupcakes completely on a wire rack before icing

# Tips for icing & decorating cupcakes

There's no need to get too complicated. Basic decoration can be just attractive as something more elaborate, but cupcakes are as much about icing and decoration as cake, so allow yourself to be as creative as you wish.

- Originally the icing for cupcakes was always level with the top of the paper cases to give a smooth top. It's trendy now to be as flamboyant and creative as possible with spiral icing and gem decoration

- For a smooth, shiny finish when icing, pour the icing on to the cake top then tip the cake so the icing naturally runs around it, filling the top, inside the paper case

- As well as shiny glaze, consider crystallised flowers, fruit, chocolates, such as crumbled Flake bars or chocolate buttons, and sparkles. Sweets are a popular choice for children's cakes

- Decorate immediately after icing – once the icing has set, you risk spoiling the look of the icing

# Raspberry Cupcakes

These raspberry cupcakes simply look stunning and can be dressed up or down to suit the occasion. Use a full blackcurrant drink for its darker colour – the light version is too pale; you could use pink food colouring instead. Makes 12 cupcakes. Store in an airtight container for up to 2 days. Freeze, un-iced, in an airtight plastic box for up to 2 months.

100 g (4 oz) fresh raspberries, reserving 12 to decorate
100 g (4 oz) baking margarine, from the fridge
100 g (4 oz) caster sugar
2 eggs
100 g (4 oz) self-raising flour
1 tsp baking powder
*For the icing*
175 g (6 oz) icing sugar
1 tbsp water
2 tbsp blackcurrant squash, not blackcurrant light

Preheat oven 180°C/160°C fan/gas 4. Line a 12-hole muffin tin with paper cases. Put the raspberries (reserving 12 to decorate) and the rest of the cake ingredients into a bowl or mixer and beat until combined and smooth. Spoon evenly into the paper cases. Bake in the preheated oven for about 20 mins until well risen and golden; in the Aga, bake on the grid shelf on the floor of the roasting oven with the cold sheet on the second set of runners for 15 mins. Leave to cool. To make the icing, put the icing sugar into a bowl and mix with the water and squash to give a smooth icing. Spoon over the cold cakes and spread to the edges. Decorate with one reserved raspberry or a crystallised rose petal.

# better brownies

These American-style teatime treats are not so much fluffy, light cakes as moist, dense, fudgy bars. You can also have them for dessert with a dollop of cream, crème fraîche or ice cream. Or cut them into tiny petits fours to have with coffee after dinner.

- The golden rule is to avoid the temptation to over-cook brownies or they will end up dry. Like gingerbread, they are likely to dip a little in the middle – this is how they should be and means that they are nicely gooey inside though crunchy on top. Remember that they firm up as they cool down

- I like to use soft brown sugar, as it adds a lovely caramel richness

- Use a traybake tin, preferably, to make it easier to cut into bars or squares

- Vanilla extract not essence is best for superior flavour – not the cheap option but you only need a little

- Bake in the centre of the oven to allow the heat to circulate around the tin

- To cut through brownies' intense sweetness, try serving them with a little crème fraîche

# Chocolate & brownies

- I have used chocolate chips for extra chocolatiness – you could replace the chocolate chips with nuts, walnuts or pecan nuts are particularly good, or dried fruit, if you prefer. If you choose nuts for a crunchy contrast, it's good to toast them a little first to bring out their flavour

- Don't allow any chocolate to get too hot or it will become lumpy when mixed with the other ingredients

- Of the brands, I find Bournville chocolate is the reliable choice as it melts and sets perfectly

- Avoid white chocolate chips – in my experience, they sink and go rock hard

## Chocolate Brownies

These brownies are especially indulgent and chocolatey. Cuts into 20 pieces. Store for up to 3 days in an airtight tin. Freeze, uncut, in a box for up to a month.

350 g (12 oz) Bournville chocolate, broken into pieces

225 g (8 oz) unsalted butter, cut into pieces

4 eggs

225 g (8 oz) soft light brown sugar

1 tsp vanilla extract

75 g (3 oz) self-raising flour

100 g (4 oz) plain chocolate chips

Preheat oven to 190°C/170°C fan/gas 5. Grease and line a traybake tin or small roasting tin about 30 x 33 cm (12 x 9 in) with foil. Melt together the chocolate and butter in a bowl set over a pan of gently simmering water until smooth and completely melted (don't allow to get too hot). Beat together the eggs, sugar and vanilla extract in a large bowl. Pour in the melted chocolate and butter, and stir. Stir in the flour and chocolate chips, and beat until smooth. Pour into the prepared tin and bake in the preheated oven for about 40–45 mins or until firm to the touch and a light crust forms on top. For Aga cooks: bake on the grid shelf on the floor of the roasting oven with the cold sheet on the second set of runners for 20 mins; transfer the now hot cold sheet to the simmering oven and sit the tin on top and bake for a further 20 mins. Once cooked, leave to cool in the tin before cutting.

# better muffins

These muffins are American-style cupcakes, though actually less sweet than cupcakes (so good for breakfast) and usually not iced (though sometimes glazed); the higher the butter and sugar content, the more cake-like the muffin. Muffins feel light for their size and have a bumpy top. By contrast, English muffins are made with yeast (not baking powder); so they are quite different and more breadlike, generally served toasted and buttered.

- The secret of light muffins is quick, gentle and light mixing; but remember that muffins are not as light as sponge cakes and should be a little more dense

- It is important to keep the mixture light so the fruit does not sink to the bottom

- Using melted butter makes for a better-flavoured muffin

- A mix of plain flour and baking powder is preferable to self-raising flour because it results in a slightly dense, less springy sponge

*small cakes & cookies*

- Look out for muffin cases (deeper) not bun cases (more shallow) – the deeper the case, the easier to extract the muffins from the tins

- Fill each case only halfway up, so the cakes keep their shape and don't balloon over the top as they rise in the oven

- Turn the tin halfway through baking for even browning

- When tops are risen, golden and spring to a light touch, and an inserted toothpick or skewer comes out clean, the muffins are cooked – don't over-bake or they will be dry

- Muffins didn't rise? Check you used the right amount of baking powder, didn't over-mix, and that the oven temperature was not too low

- Best eaten warm – especially for breakfast – and because they are low in fat and don't store well, also best on the day they are made. Otherwise keep in the fridge

- Mini muffins are just the right size for small children – the recipe below will make 24 mini muffins, which should be cooked for slightly less time

## Blueberry Breakfast Muffins

These muffins are similar to scones in texture and so perfect for breakfast. Instead of the blueberries, you could use nuts, chocolate or dried fruit – muffins are versatile. Makes 12 muffins. Store in the fridge in an airtight tin or poly bag for up to 2 days. Freeze for up to a month then thaw for 3 hours and reheat for about 5 mins in a moderate oven (180°C/fan 160°C/gas 4) to serve warm.

300 g (10 oz) plain flour
1 tbsp baking powder
75 g (3 oz) caster sugar
grated zest of 1 lemon
2 eggs
225 ml (8 fl oz) milk
100 g (4 oz) butter, melted and left to cool
1 tsp vanilla extract
225 g (8 oz) fresh blueberries
a little demerara sugar, for sprinkling (optional)

Preheat oven to 200°C/fan 180°C/gas 6. Measure the flour, baking powder, sugar and grated zest into a mixing bowl and stir briefly. Mix together the eggs, milk, butter and vanilla extract then add these to the dry ingredients. Mix together the ingredients with a wooden spoon or spatula, but don't over-mix. Gently stir in the blueberries and spoon the mixture into a greased (or lined with paper cases) 12-hole muffin tin, filling each one almost to the top. Sprinkle each muffin with the demerara sugar, if using. Bake in the preheated oven for 20–25 mins until golden brown. For Aga cooks: bake on the grid shelf on the floor of the roasting oven with the cold sheet on the second set of runners for 20 mins. Allow to cool slightly in the tin on a wire cooling rack then lift out and serve warm.

# better cookies

A cookie is a chewy biscuit; in America, where cookies are an institution, they are twinned with Christmas – traditionally given as presents, built into cookie houses and strung decoratively around on strings. But, fortunately, cookies are not just for Christmas …

- Adding half soft brown sugar helps give a gooey centre (but use all caster sugar, if you prefer)

- Mixing cookies should be quick and easy – just mix until combined and don't over-beat otherwise they will be flat and oily

- You can prepare cookie dough and keep it covered for up to 6 hours in the fridge until you are ready to bake – or freeze, well wrapped in a plastic bag for up to a month

- Put the spoonfuls of cookie dough a little apart on the baking sheet so they have room to spread as they cook

- Bake on any shelf in a fan oven and otherwise in the centre

- If you bake more than one tray of cookies at once, the cooking time may be a minute or so longer

- Turn the baking sheets halfway through baking so they bake evenly

- Cooked? They should be slightly darker around the edge with a centre that is soft but not oily – golden rule: under-bake rather than over-bake

- Don't worry if your cookies look too soft at first – they firm up as they cool

- Remove from the oven immediately they are cooked or they will quickly go hard

- On taking from the oven, let the cookies sit in the tin for a couple of minutes to firm up a little so they are easier to remove. Then transfer carefully, using a palette knife or fish slice, to a wire cooling rack and leave until completely cold

- Store cookies in an airtight, tightly lidded plastic container – the idea is to keep them soft and chewy and not to let them go hard like a biscuit

- You can also store in a container in the fridge, so they stay moist and soggy (you would not do this with a biscuit)

- To restore freshness to dried-out or limp cookies, reheat them briefly in a cool oven (150°C/fan 130°C/gas 2) before serving

## Chocolate Chip Cookies

This delicious cookie has a little extra essential gooeyness from the flakes of nougat in the Toblerone. Makes 18 cookies. Store, well wrapped, for 3 days. Freeze cooked in a freezer bag or box for up to a month (the raw cookie mixture freezes well, too, for up to a month).

75 g (3 oz) butter, plus extra for greasing
75 g (3 oz) caster sugar
75 g (3 oz) soft brown sugar
1 egg, beaten
175 g (6 oz) plain flour
1 x 100 g bar milk Toblerone, roughly chopped into raisin-sized pieces

Preheat oven to 180°C/fan 160°C/gas 4. Grease three baking sheets with butter (or grease one and bake in batches). Cream the butter and sugars in a mixing bowl until light and fluffy. Beat in the egg, flour and Toblerone. Spoon six large teaspoonfuls on to each baking sheet, spaced well apart as the cookies spread as they cook. Bake in the preheated oven for 15–18 mins until golden brown; in the Aga, slide on to the grid shelf on the floor of the roasting oven with the cold sheet on the second set of runners for about 10 mins. After a couple mins of cooling out of the oven, carefully transfer to a wire rack.

# classic cakes

Better Fruit Cakes

Better Chocolate Cakes

Better Meringues

Better Biscuits

Better Scones

Some teatime treats are national treasures – all of the ones that feature in this chapter have a long pedigree. These are the teatime treats that have stood the test of time and emerged our favourites. Some more traditional ones often have more ingredients and longer baking methods than the new arrivals, so I have brought them up to date by introducing new flavours and techniques, making them just as delicious but simpler to make and bake.

# better fruit cakes

Fruit cakes are celebratory; tradition requires a proper fruit cake, something beautifully moist and rich, iced for Christmas or other celebrations. But fruit cake is equally good served plain at any time of the year. Which fruit? You decide – but make sure it equals the quantity specified in the recipe.

- Make a minimum 1 month (and up to 6 months) ahead, so the fruit and sponge have the chance to firm up before you want to eat it, and the cake won't crumble when cut

- Most fruit cakes are invariably equal amounts of butter, sugar and flour, and an egg for every 50 g (2 oz) butter. Extra flour is sometimes added to balance out a liquid ingredient such as fruit juice or alcohol

- If using fruit in syrup, e.g. cherries or ginger, be sure to wash off the syrup and dry well

- Creaming the butter and the sugar well, so it's light and fluffy, is crucial – the fruit needs to suspend in a good sponge mixture

- When you spoon the raw mixture into the tin, it should have a slow dropping consistency, similar to clotted cream

- If you are in a hurry, a dense fruit cake can be made in its tin and before baking kept covered in cling film in a cool place until you are ready to bake (or up to 24 hours) – because of the high quantity of fruit it cannot sink or lose volume

- A fruit cake's lengthy cooking time means that it benefits from a heavy-based tin to avoid scorching; one with a removable base so that it is easier to remove from the tin, though a springform tin works well too

- Recipes for fruit cake used to insist we line the cake tin three times with greaseproof paper to protect the cake from burning. Now with fan ovens and lower cooking temperatures it is not so important, so just line once

- Bake in the centre of the oven or, if you have an Aga, in the simmering oven

- Check after 2 hours or so – if the cake is a perfect dark golden colour, then cover with foil to stop it turning darker or burning

- To test when cooked, insert a skewer into the centre of the cake – if it comes out clean, the cake is cooked

- If you wrap a dense fruit cake, such as a Christmas cake, in baking parchment then foil or cling film (it must be that way round to avoid any possible reaction between the metal foil and any acid in the cake), it can be kept in the fridge or a dry, cool place for up to 6 months. Don't store in a warm place or the cake will turn mouldy

- If you're storing your cake for a period of time, once a week or so, turn it upside down and skewer through it at regular intervals. Then pour brandy into the skewer holes – just enough to soak in to keep it moist and full of flavour

- Glazed fruits or nuts make a good alternative to traditional icing

- Always cut a fruit cake with a non-serrated knife otherwise it will crumble

## *Boozy Fruit Cake*

As the name suggests, this fruit cake is boozy enough, so there is no need to feed it with alcohol once made. Cuts into 10–12 wedges. Store wrapped in baking parchment and foil/cling film for up to 6 months in a cool place. Freezes well, un-iced, wrapped in cling film and foil, for up to 6 months.

225 g (8 oz) butter, softened

225 g (8 oz) light muscovado sugar

225 g (8 oz) plain flour

4 eggs

90 ml (3½ fl oz) dark rum

225 g (8 oz) raisins

450 g (1 lb) sultanas

225 g (8 oz) dried cranberries

175 g (6 oz) glacé cherries, rinsed, dried and cut into quarters

175 g (6 oz) dried apricots, cut into raisin-size pieces

Preheat oven to 140°C/fan 120°C/gas 1. Grease a deep 20 cm (8 in) cake tin and base line with non-stick baking parchment. Measure the butter and sugar into a large mixing bowl, and cream with a wooden spoon. Add the rest of the ingredients and continue to mix until combined. Spoon the mix into the prepared tin and spread out evenly with the back of a spoon. Bake in the preheated oven for 4–4½ hours. Check after 2 hours, and if the cake is a perfect rich dark golden colour, cover with foil. In the Aga, bake in the simmering oven for 6–9 hours until rich, dark and golden. Leave to cool in the tin then remove and store, as above, until needed. Decorate with traditional icing or glazed fruits.

# better chocolate cakes

When it comes to indulgence, chocolate cake is tops.

## *A word about chocolate*

Chocolate comes in many flavours and forms: plain, also known as dark, milk or white; block or chips. Chocolate that is particularly suitable for baking can be found in supermarket baking sections, near the flour and sugar.

*Plain chocolate, also known as dark chocolate* For general baking I avoid 70 per cent cocoa solid chocolate as it is sometimes less successful when it comes to setting as it is too soft.

> *If making truffles you must use a chocolate that has 70 per cent cocoa solids, so they are soft to eat*

*White chocolate* I always use 100 per cent Belgian white chocolate – this melts perfectly and is virtually foolproof. Some otherwise excellent white chocolates that are great for eating just don't melt; rather, they separate and are therefore unsuited to baking.

*Do not over-heat white chocolate or it may split*

*Chocolate or plain chocolate chips in packets* – try the dark ones as they have the stronger chocolate flavour.

*To melt* break into chunks into a bowl and sit carefully over a pan of just hot, simmering water – the steam will melt the chocolate. Also melts perfectly on the back of the Aga.

*Drinking chocolate* vs *cocoa powder* Cocoa gives cakes the most intense, chocolatey flavour

# Foolproof Chocolate Cake

This chocolate cake is simply made via the all-in-one method. I have named it with care, because I promise perfection here. Cuts into 6–8 wedges. Store iced in the fridge for 2 days but be aware the icing will lose its shine if kept in the fridge, so, ideally, ice on the day. Freeze un-iced, wrapped in cling film and foil or in a box, for up to a month.

*for the cake*
100 g (4 oz) self-raising flour
25 g (1 oz) cocoa powder
1 tsp baking powder
100 g (4 oz) caster sugar
6 tbsp sunflower oil
3 tbsp milk
2 eggs
*for the fudge icing*
25 g (1 oz) butter
1 tbsp cocoa powder
about 1 tbsp milk
100 g (4 oz) icing sugar, sifted, plus extra for dusting
a little warmed strawberry jam

Preheat oven to 180°C/fan160°C/gas 4. Grease and base line with a disc of baking parchment a 20 cm (8 in) loose-bottomed cake tin. Put the flour, cocoa, baking powder and sugar into a mixing bowl. Pour the oil, milk and eggs into a jug and beat together with a fork, and pour into the flour mix. Beat with a wooden spoon or electric hand whisk till smooth. Spoon into the prepared tin and level the top. Bake in the preheated oven for about 30 mins; in the Aga, on the grid shelf on the floor of the roasting oven with the cold sheet on the second set of runners for 25 mins. Leave to cool in the tin then turn out and remove the baking parchment.

To make the fudge icing, melt the butter in a small pan, add the cocoa and cook for a minute. Remove from the heat and stir in the milk and icing sugar. Beat well with a wooden spoon till smooth then set aside to thicken for about 10 mins till a spreading consistency. Spread the top of the cake with the warmed jam then spread the fudge icing over the top and sides, and dust with icing sugar to serve.

# better meringues

Meringues are made from egg white and sugar – and lots of air incorporated during whisking. Soft meringues are used for toppings, such as for lemon meringue pie; individual firm meringues are baked for longer at a lower temperature and have a crunchy shell and are like candyfloss inside. In spite of a reputation for being difficult, making your own meringues is not complicated and a great string to have to your bow. However, you will need an electric hand whisk or a free-standing mixer to whisk the egg whites as they take too long to make by hand.

- Make sure there is no egg yolk in the egg whites or they will not whisk successfully

- Separate the yolks from the whites one by one into a small bowl first, then transfer each white to the whisking bowl, so that if you do have an accident and add some yolk, you won't lose the lot

- The ratio is always one egg white per 50 g (2 oz) caster sugar

- Use only caster sugar for meringues – granulated sugar gives a speckled, crunchy meringue and may sink to the bottom and result in a sticky base

- For brown meringues, use three-quarters caster sugar and one-third soft fine brown sugar

- Use eggs straight from the fridge or at room temperature, a few days old or fresh – it makes no difference; they just whip up a bit faster at room temperature

- Use a free-standing mixer for ease. Or an electric hand whisk in a large bowl, but it will take longer to make up (up to about 10 mins) as the whisks are smaller than on a machine

- Do not use a machine with a lid because the idea is to get air into the egg whites

- Don't over whisk the whites – just to stiff peaks – or they will turn liquid

- Don't add the sugar too soon or you'll knock the air out of the egg whites. Instead, add it once the whites are as stiff as they can get and then add the sugar gradually, a teaspoon at a time, still whisking hard. This is the secret, as the sugar will then stay suspended in the whites

- To fill a piping bag, roll down the sides of the bag (as you would when putting on your stockings), then fill it or sit it in a jug, and it will be easier to fill and won't go everywhere. As it fills up, just roll the sides up higher

- If the meringues don't come off the paper easily after 50 minutes, it means they are not completely cooked, so return to the oven until they easily detach

- Some meringues benefit from filling with cream ahead of time as this slightly softens the centre while leaving the outside crisp. For example, pavlovas and large meringues can be filled up to 8 hours ahead – if you like a soft centre, as I do

# Teeny-Weeny Meringues

Serving meringues for tea is quite old fashioned but rather smart. These bite-size ones are so easy to eat and therefore perfect finger food for parties. Makes about 30 meringues. Store cooked meringues wrapped in a sealed plastic bag or box in a cool place for up to 2 months. Put in an airtight box to freeze, for up to 4 months, taking care because they crush easily. *Ideally, you will need a piping bag and 5 mm (¼ in) plain nozzle for piping the meringues (though they can be made without piping, as below).*

*for the meringues*
4 egg whites
225 g (8 oz) caster sugar
*for the filling*
150 ml (¼ pint) double cream, whipped
a few fresh raspberries or strawberries

Preheat oven to140°C/fan120°C/gas 1. Grease and line a baking sheet with non-stick baking parchment. Put the egg whites into a large bowl (or the bowl of a free-standing mixer). Whisk with an electric hand whisk (or the tabletop mixer) on a high speed until white and fluffy, like a cloud. Still whisking on maximum speed, gradually add the sugar, a teaspoon at a time, until incorporated and the meringue is stiff and shiny, and stands upright on the whisk. Spoon the meringue into the piping bag fitted with the nozzle, and pipe a very small circle (about the size of £2 coin). Then pipe again around the edge of the circle in one layer – to make a little nest. Continue piping more nests until you have used up all the meringue. If you are not keen on piping, spoon teaspoonfuls on to the baking parchment and use the back of the spoon to make an indent or nest in the centre of each meringue. Bake in the preheated oven for about 45 mins; in an Aga, in the simmering oven for up to 50 mins. Remove the meringues from the baking parchment on to a wire rack and set aside until stone cold. Spoon a little whipped cream into the centre of each nest and top with a raspberry or quarter strawberry. Keep in the fridge until ready to serve – filled meringues will keep in the fridge for up to 3 hours.

# better biscuits

Biscuits are the crisp side of the cookie–biscuit family.

- Biscuits can be tricky to bake because of their high proportion of sugar, so watch them carefully as they are prone to burning

- To check when cooked, biscuits should be slightly darker around the edge with a centre that is soft but not oily

- Don't worry if your biscuits aren't crisp at first – they crisp up as they cool

- After removing biscuits from the oven, leave them for about 10 mins to firm up on the baking sheet. Then, carefully remove with a palette knife or fish slice on to a wire cooling rack and leave until completely cold

- Store and freeze biscuits layered in kitchen paper to keep them crisp – the paper absorbs the moisture and stops the biscuits becoming soft

- Be sure to eat any biscuits that contain egg or fresh fruit within a couple of days because they don't keep – otherwise you can freeze them

- Some biscuits may need refreshing on defrosting – arrange them flat on a baking sheet in a single layer and bake at 150°C/fan130°C/gas 2 for 5 mins; in the Aga, in the simmering oven for 8–10 minutes

# better shortbread

This sweet Scottish crumbly biscuit is traditionally made with lots of butter and baked in a round tin.

- Semolina gives shortbread a lovely crunch – or use cornflour instead

- Always use butter for that essential melt-in-the-mouth texture that gives the best flavour

- Especially if making by hand, don't over-mix or the heat of your hands may make the fat oily – the raw mixture should be fairly dry to give a short texture

- Don't bother to grease or line the tin before baking – the large quantity of butter stops any sticking

- Prick with a fork before baking so it doesn't rise in the centre

- Dusting with a sprinkling of caster sugar, usually after baking, is traditional, but I suggest sprinkling with demerara sugar before baking to give a nice golden crunch

- Bake until firm in the centre and very pale golden – don't over-bake to golden brown or it will end up being too crisp and dry

- Cut into wedges in the tin after a brief initial cooling then allow to cool completely in the tin before removing to a wire rack

# Scottish Shortbread

An unbeatably buttery biscuit. Makes 12 wedges. Store in a tin lined with kitchen paper for up to 3 days. Freeze the cut shortbread biscuits in a plastic box lined with kitchen paper and store for up to 2 months.

175 g (6 oz) plain flour
175 g (6 oz) butter, at room temperature
75 g (3 oz) caster sugar
75 g (3 oz) semolina
a little demerara sugar, for sprinkling

Preheat oven to 160°C/fan140°C/gas 3. In a food processor, thoroughly combine the flour, butter, sugar and semolina until the mixture comes together to form a dough. Or, by hand, rub the butter into the flour then add the sugar and semolina, and work together the ingredients to form a ball. Press half the dough into a round 20 cm (8 in) cake tin and level with the back of a spoon. Sprinkle with demerara sugar. Bake in the preheated oven for 30–40 mins; in the Aga, slide on to the lowest set of runners in the roasting oven with the cold sheet on the second set of runners for 20 mins then transfer to the simmering oven for a further

*classic cakes*

45 mins. Cool in the tin for a few mins then cut into 12 wedges and leave to cool in the tin until stone cold.

# better scones

Another British classic, scones are generally small and round, and made from a soft dough baked in a hot oven.

- A slightly wetter than drier dough is best when making scones as it rises better

- Knead well so the dough is completely smooth before cutting

- Any dough trimmings can be kneaded again until smooth and re-shaped ready to cut again

- When cutting scones with a scone cutter, do not twist the cutter or the scone will be uneven in height and therefore not rise evenly

- I believe there's no need to butter scones if you're using cream – just strawberry or raspberry jam is ideal

- The correct way to eat a scone is to break it in half with your fingers – don't cut it with a knife (another advantage of these mini scones)

- Children love making scones as they are easy to mix and the kneading is great fun

- Scones are versatile – they can be sweet (with fresh or dried fruit or spices) or savoury (with cheese or herbs, so they go perfectly with soup or pâté)

## *Mini Scones*

These scones are small and perfect for eating while standing up, as they just pop in the mouth in one go. Makes 22 scones. Store in a bag in the fridge for up to 2 days but best eaten fresh. Freeze in a sealed bag for up to a month. *You will need a 2 cm (1 in) fluted scone cutter.*

225 g (8 oz) self-raising flour
2 tsp baking powder
40 g (1½ oz) butter, softened, plus extra for greasing
25 g (1 oz) caster sugar
1 egg
about 150 ml (¼ pint) milk

Preheat oven to 200°C/fan180°C/gas 6. Grease a baking sheet. Mix to breadcrumbs the flour, baking powder, sugar and butter in a free-standing mixer or food processor. In a measuring jug, beat an egg with a fork and pour in enough milk to make 150 ml (¼ pint), then beat again to mix. Turn on the machine and gradually pour in the milk and egg, leaving about a tablespoon for glazing. Whiz until combined to a slightly sticky mixture. Knead the dough on a floured work surface until smooth. Roll with a rolling pin to about 1 cm (½ in) thick then cut out the scones with the scone cutter. Re-roll the remaining dough and cut out more scones; repeat until all the dough is used. Arrange the scones on the greased baking sheet and brush the top of each with the reserved egg and milk mixture. Bake in the preheated oven for 10–12 mins until well risen and golden brown; in the Aga, on the floor of the roasting oven for 10 mins. Transfer to a wire cooling rack. Once cold, break in half and top each half with clotted cream and strawberry jam to serve.

# healthy cakes

Baking with fruit & veg

Baking with nuts & seeds

Dairy-free cakes

Using wholemeal flour

We are all more health conscious now – but there's no need to deny ourselves teatime treats or elevenses with this selection of wholesome, guilt-free options plus a few tips on how to bake for maximum health.

# baking with fruit & veg

Fruit cakes are the ultimate in making cakes with fruit, but there are other roles for fruit and vegetables in baking. Here are some fruit bowl, vegetable basket and storecupboard stand-bys and tips on how to use them.

*Most cakes made with fresh fruit or vegetables keep only for a short time, as they easily turn mouldy – so eat within a day or two or freeze*

## *Fruit*

**Apples** Cooking apples are softer than dessert apples and lose their shape more easily than eating apples when cooked. Use sliced, diced or grated – dried apple is available too

**Apricots** If using dried apricots, the dried ready-to-eat variety avoids having to soak the fruit in liquid before use. They come in two shades: natural is slightly darker than the bright orange alternative – either works just as well.

**Bananas** If you have some over-ripe bananas sitting in the fruit bowl, they are perfect for baking into breads or cakes, with dried fruit or chocolate, if you like. You can also buy dried bananas, which are good in fruit cakes or for flavouring in custards.

**Blueberries** and other fresh soft fruit, such as raspberries and strawberries, work well in muffins and cupcakes and are good for decorating. Polish them off quickly, though, because the fresh fruit doesn't keep well and soon becomes wilted and mouldy.

**Citrus fruits** Lemons, oranges and limes are baking staples, especially the zest and juice. If zesting, try to buy unwaxed fruit. Use a fine grater to remove the zest or a zester that will give the long, thin strips that are perfect for decoration; pare the zest for infusing in milk.

**Crystallised fruit,** such as slices of lemon, lime or orange, or crystallised soft fruit, is good for cake decoration. You can buy it from supermarkets or kitchen shops or make your own.

*healthy cakes*

*How to crystallise your own soft fruit or edible flowers* Brush soft fruit, e.g. blueberries, or flowers, such as primroses, with egg white and carefully dip in caster sugar. Leave to set on a cooling rack or on baking parchment in a warm place – an airing cupboard or back of the Aga – until the sugar crystallises and sets firm on the fruit and flowers, giving a perfect decoration for a variety of cakes (primroses are perfect for simnel cakes).

Alternatively, why not use fresh fruit, such as strawberries and raspberries, half dipped in melted white or plain chocolate and arrange on baking parchment to set hard.

**Dates** High in sugar and intensely sweet; the best for baking are the dried, pitted ones – perfect for fruit cake and a good match with bananas.

**Glacé cherries** If you can find the dark red, natural-coloured glacé cherries rather than the fake-colouring bright red ones, all the better. Wash off the syrup and dry well before adding to a sponge mixture.

**Stem or preserved ginger** Made from the stem of tender young ginger, and it keeps well, even when opened. Great added chopped to cakes and biscuits. Use the ginger syrup in which the preserved stem ginger sits when a recipe specifies ginger syrup.

**Dried fruit** Not just raisins, sultanas and currants but also figs, cranberries, prunes, mangoes and pears. Mixed dried fruit in bags – often called fruit medley or tropical fruit medley – makes for a sweeter flavour and adds lots of lovely colour. Dried fruit often benefits from soaking before use, such as in alcohol or tea (for teabreads).

**Tinned fruit** Drain and dry all tinned fruit, such as crushed pineapple, or the excess moisture will make the fruit sink to the bottom of the cake.

**Jam & marmalade** If you're adding either to the cake mixture, don't be tempted to put in too much as this alters the proportion of the sugar and can result in a less than successful cake. Spreading the top and middle of a cake with jam keeps it moist and prevents the crumbs from mixing with the icing. Warming jam or marmalade makes it easier to spread. Bought jams can be firmer set than homemade ones, so can sometimes be tricky to melt for covering a cake or glazing; if so, add a little water or lemon juice when melting, whisk until smooth and you will find this is easier to spread.

## Vegetables

**Beetroot** Popular, pre-cooked, for cakes – the colour is a stunning bright red and the flavour quite sweet.

**Carrots** Contain more sugar than any other veg apart from sugar beet! They have been used to sweeten cakes for centuries. Baking really brings out their sweetness, adds colour, flavour and texture, and helps keep cakes moist as the carrots soften during baking.

**Courgettes** You'll get the best results with small courgettes, as large ones can be too wet. Don't peel them – it's best to keep on the green skin so that they hold their shape and you can see the colour.

**Pumpkins** Useful in baking with their earthy sweetness and dense, fibrous texture. You'll find them added to cakes and muffins, scones and pies – the pumpkin adds moistness and texture as well as colour. It's often cooked and puréed before use, and goes well with spices like cinnamon and ginger.

## Nuts & seeds

Whole, flaked or ground, or even nut butters, nut are generally nutritious – full of protein, vitamins and minerals – but high in carbohydrates and oils, so don't overdo them. Always use nuts within their use-by date or they might make your cakes taste rancid. Also make sure you store them in cool, dry, dark conditions in an airtight container, once opened, to keep them fresh.

*I keep my nuts in the freezer to prevent them turning rancid – use straight from the freezer as they defrost in minutes*

**Almonds** Especially nutritious and also contain iron, calcium, vitamins B2 and E and zinc; ground almonds especially help to keep cake texture moist; almond slithers are attractively sliced whole almonds but you can carefully cut your own from whole almonds or use flaked almonds instead.

**Brazil nuts** are not only very high in protein (as well as iron, calcium and zinc) but also in fat, so they tend to turn rancid quickly.

**Coconut** Especially useful is *desiccated coconut*, which adds fine texture to cakes. Along with *flaked coconut*, which is good for decoration, it can be found near the dried fruits in supermarkets.

**Hazelnuts** If you're short of time, buy roasted, chopped hazelnuts – otherwise buy whole roasted ones and chop finely; hazelnuts are lower in fat than most nuts.

**Macadamia nuts** Expensive but add a crunchy texture and creamy flavour; low carbohydrate, but high fat.

**Peanuts** Relatively inexpensive, so think about mixing them with other nuts for economy – good for biscuits and cookies; contain protein, iron and zinc.

**Pine nuts** Good for using in biscuits as they hold their shape; they turn rancid easily so should be stored in a fridge or freezer.

**Pistachio nuts** Contain iron and calcium; be aware that the nuts can turn soft and waxy when baked, not good if what you're after is nutty crunch.

**Pecan nuts** Great toasted in brownies; they taste like a mild, sweet walnut, and are very high in fat and vitamin A, and contain iron and calcium. They look very attractive glazed on fruit cakes.

**Walnuts** Watch out because walnuts are very high in fat and quickly turn rancid, so perhaps store in the fridge or freezer; they are a good source of iron and fabulous in brownies and coffee cake and for decoration.

**Note on roasting nuts** To bring out the true flavour it is good to toast nuts before baking with them. Nuts contain a high proportion of oil, so can burn easily – for this reason I toast them in a non-stick frying pan over a low heat on the hob – watching carefully and turning them, until a golden brown – they turn brown within a couple of mins.

**Seeds** pack a powerful health punch and are a good source of protein; in particular, *pumpkin seeds* are rich in iron, zinc and phosphorous as well as calcium and magnesium; *sunflower seeds* are high in potassium and phosphorous and contain iron and calcium; unhulled or whole *sesame seeds* are especially high in calcium, manganese and copper, so look out for them; *black poppy seeds* are great, in lemon cakes and sprinkled over a pale icing, for decoration.

# Carrot & Walnut Cake

A classic carrot cake with a walnut twist – delicious and wholesome. Cuts into 8 wedges. Store in the fridge for up to 2 days. Freezes well, un-iced, wrapped in foil for up to 1 month.

- Using carrots is not only good for your 5-a-day but also helps to keep the cake moist – carrot cake should be soft and dense

- Coarsely grate carrots so they hold their shape, finely grated they will make the cake too wet

- I often add milk when using wholemeal flour, which is quite absorbent and can otherwise result in a drier cake

- Don't worry if the raw mixture is quite stiff – that's what's needed to hold the walnuts and carrots in place and stop them sinking

- Carrot cake is good plain but is often iced, usually with white or soft cheese icing, as here – and you can keep it healthy and less loaded with calories by using low-fat soft cheese. Full-fat works well too. Because this icing is dairy you will need to keep the iced cake in the fridge

- If you love icing, although a little less healthy, as a variation you could make this cake in two 20 cm sandwich tins and bake for 25 mins. Double the icing and use the extra to sandwich the cakes together and then ice on top

*for the cake*
150 ml (¼ pint) sunflower oil
250 g (9 oz) wholemeal self-raising flour
1 tsp baking powder
150 g (5 oz) light muscovado sugar
1 tsp vanilla extract
50 g (2 oz) walnuts, shelled and coarsely chopped
150 g (5 oz) carrots, peeled and coarsely grated
2 eggs
2 tbsp milk
*for the icing*
225 g (8 oz) low-fat soft cheese
2 tbsp icing sugar
1 tsp vanilla extract

Preheat oven 180°C/fan160°C/gas 4. Grease and base line a deep 20 cm (8 in) cake tin with non-stick baking parchment. Put all the cake ingredients into a large bowl and mix firmly with a wooden spoon until combined. Spoon into the prepared tin and level the top. Bake in the preheated oven for about 45 mins until golden brown and firm to the touch and a skewer inserted into the centre of the cake comes out clean; in an Aga, slide on to the grid shelf on the floor of the roasting oven with the cold sheet on the second set of runners for 25 mins. Transfer the now hot cold sheet into the simmering oven, sit the cake on top and bake for a further 15 mins. Set aside to cool. To ice: mix together all the icing ingredients and spread over the cold cake.

## *Apple Dairy-free Fruit Loaf*

Traditional healthy baking at its best, and this fruit loaf is moist and full of fruit. Cuts into 6–8 slices. Store in a cake tin or in the fridge for up to a week. Freeze, wrapped in foil, for up to 2 months.

- A dairy- and sugar-free cake – but at no cost to taste

- Prunes are very healthy with their high levels of fibre, essential minerals and antioxidants – they are also fat-free

- Apple juice is a healthy liquid sweetener – you can use the sort that you would drink for breakfast

- You can replace the dried apples and pears here with a packet of tropical fruit medley or similar, if you wish

- As this cake is so dense with fruit, the skewer test is the best way to be sure that it's cooked

75 g (3 oz) dried stoned prunes, roughly chopped
150 ml (¼ pint) boiling water
100 g (4 oz) self-raising flour
½ tsp baking powder
½ tsp ground mixed spice
75 g (3 oz) dried apples, chopped into large pieces
75 g (3 oz) dried apricots, chopped into large pieces
50 g (2 oz) dried pears, chopped into large pieces
50 g (2 oz) sultanas
3 tbsp apple juice
a little demerara sugar, for sprinkling

Grease and line a 450 g (1 lb) loaf tin with non-stick baking parchment. Put the prunes into a heatproof bowl and pour over boiling water. Set aside for about 1 hour to plump up and cool down, after which, preheat oven to 180°C/fan160°C/gas 4. Put the rest of the ingredients, apart from the demerara sugar, into a mixing bowl and stir until smooth. Fold in the prunes and their soaking water. Spoon into the prepared tin, level the top and sprinkle with the demerara sugar. Bake in the preheated oven for about 1 hour 10 mins, until golden brown and a skewer comes out clean when inserted into the centre of the cake. For Aga cooks, put a small grill rack inside a small roasting tin and sit the tin on top and bake on the grid shelf on the floor of the roasting oven with the cold sheet on the second set of runners for about an hour. Set aside to cool and turn out of the tin.

## Seeded Fruit Bars

These not only look good but you also know they are doing you good as you eat them, with this health-boost of oats, seeds and dried fruit. Makes 18 bars. Store in a cake tin or in the fridge for up to 4 days. Unsuitable for freezing.

• Use porridge oats not jumbo oats as they absorb flavours and mix more readily with the other ingredients

- Oats have a low GI or glycaemic index, which means they release energy slowly, making them the healthy option

- For a sweet flavour and jewel colours, I like to use a fruit medley or tropical fruit medley for this recipe – you could use the same quantity of sultanas, currants or raisins, if you prefer

- Dried fruit, particularly apricots, peaches and figs, are a good source of iron

- Perfect for a post-gym treat

100 g (4 oz) butter, plus extra for greasing
100 g (4 oz) light soft brown sugar
75 g (3 oz) golden syrup
200 g (8 oz) porridge oats
50 g (2 oz) pumpkin seeds
50 g (2 oz) sunflower seeds
25 g (1 oz) sesame seeds
175 g (6 oz) dried fruit, such as apricots, peaches, apples, pears, mangoes and pineapples, cut into sultana-size pieces

Preheat oven to 160°C/fan140°C/gas 3. Grease and line sides and base of a 30 x 23 cm/12 x 9 in traybake tin with non-stick baking parchment. Heat the butter, sugar and golden syrup in a pan over a low heat, until the butter has melted and the sugar dissolved. Put the oats and seeds into a mixing bowl, add the chopped dried fruit and pour over the warm butter mixture. Stir until combined and the dry ingredients are coated. Spoon into the prepared tin and level with the back of a spoon. Bake in the preheated oven for 20–25 mins until golden brown; in an Aga, slide on to the grid shelf on the floor of the roasting oven with the cold sheet on the second set of runners for about 15–20 mins. Set aside in the tin until lukewarm then tip out on to a board and cut into slices. Transfer to a wire rack to cool.

## *Wholemeal Cranberry Rock Cakes*

Rock cakes are all but forgotten, and I should like to revive these stalwarts of teatime and elevenses – best enjoyed split and buttered like a scone. They fill a vital role in the cake family, in that they are not generally as sweet as the more fashionable cakey delights of cupcakes and brownies, but more like a scone, though mostly larger and therefore more substantial. Makes 12 rock cakes. Store in a tin or fridge for up to 4 days. Freeze in a bag for up to 1 month.

- Essentially inexpensive, easy to make and filling

- Rock cakes should be hard and crisp, hence the name, and not soft in the centre

- With half wholemeal plain flour, my version is healthy too (though you can use all white self-raising flour, if you wish)

- Cranberries are a valuable source of vitamin C, minerals and fibre, as well as anti-ageing antioxidants; also said to offer bacterial protection as well as help with lowering cholesterol levels. Look out for dried cranberries that are sugar free

- If you like, you can replace the cranberries with other dried fruits, such as raisins, and add a little spice such as ground cinnamon or mixed spice

- The wholemeal flour can make the raw mixture somewhat drier than normal, so you may need to add a drop more milk to the mix when beating

- I use a teaspoon to spoon a good heaped dollop of the mixture on to the baking sheet, so all the rock cakes end up a similar size and therefore cook evenly

- You can also make mini rock cakes for children's parties – though slightly reduce the cooking time, as they will take less time to cook

- The light encrusting of sugar is traditional – I like demerara for its crunchier crunch

100 g (4 oz) self-raising flour
100 g (4 oz) wholemeal plain flour
2 tsp baking powder
100 g (4 oz) butter, softened, plus extra for greasing
50 g (2 oz) light muscovado sugar
100 g (4 oz) dried cranberries, snipped in half
1 egg
about 2 tbsp milk
a little demerara sugar, for sprinkling

Preheat oven to 200°C/fan180°C/gas 6 and grease a large baking sheet with butter. Put the flours and baking powder into a mixing bowl. Rub in the butter until it resembles breadcrumbs. Stir in the sugar and cranberries. In a separate bowl, whisk together the egg and milk with a fork, and pour on to the breadcrumb-like mix, mixing together gently until combined. If the mixture is a little dry, add a drop more milk. Using a teaspoon, dollop 12 rough mounds of a similar size on to the baking sheet and sprinkle each one with some demerara sugar. Bake in the preheated oven for 12–15 mins until golden brown and cooked through; in the Aga, on the grid shelf on the floor of the roasting oven with the cold sheet on the second set of runners for about 10–12 mins. Transfer to a wire rack to cool.

# kids' cakes

No-bake fridge cakes

Quick & easy fairy cakes

Fun, family cakes & biscuits

Many of my friends ask me for cakes they can make with their children: essentially fast, easy and fun. These recipes are just that, so your kids can not only enjoy learning to bake but also eat what they make before boredom sets in.

# better baking with kids

- Why not turn baking into family fun – what you and the kids can do in the kitchen together

- Prepare for sticky fingers at best

- Start with some stirring or licking out the bowl to spark interest

- Move on to cutting out biscuits and icing/decorating

- No-cook baking is a good, safe place to start

- Choose recipes that are quick to make to avoid the distractions of DVDs, Lego and so on

- Hold attention with quirky shapes, like baking stars or gingerbread men, and encourage creative icing

- Keep it low key – nothing more than a mixing bowl and a wooden spoon (and some biscuit cutters for the gingerbread men)

- Once a child has learnt a recipe, it becomes something to be proud of – so not just entertaining but good for self-esteem too

## *No-bake Chocolate Fridge Squares*

When I ask friends for favourite recipes, nearly everyone mentions fridge biscuits. They evoke memories from my own childhood – we adored making them – and your kids will too. Makes 24 squares. Store in an airtight tin in the fridge for up to a week. Unsuitable for freezing.

- Crush the biscuits finely – if the crumbs are too coarse, the squares will crumble

- For variety, replace the plain chocolate with white chocolate – Belgian white chocolate is the best for melting, in my experience

200 g (7 oz) plain chocolate, broken into pieces
450 g (1 lb) plain digestive biscuits
225 g (8 oz) butter
50 g (2 oz) caster sugar
2 tbsp golden syrup
4 tbsp cocoa powder

Grease a 30 x 23 cm (12 x 9 in) roasting tin. Put the biscuits into a plastic bag and bash with a rolling pin until they are fairly fine. Mix the butter, sugar and golden syrup in a pan over a low heat until the butter has melted. Stir in the crushed biscuits and cocoa, and mix with a wooden spoon until all the biscuits are coated. Tip into the prepared tin, spread out evenly and leave to chill in the fridge for 15 mins. Melt the chocolate in a bowl set over a pan of simmering water. Pour the melted chocolate evenly over the top of the biscuits and return to the fridge for about 1 hour or enough time for the chocolate to set. Cut into squares as required.

# Quick Fairy Cakes

Fairy cakes equal party time – and these are perennial party pieces. Makes 12 fairy cakes. Store in a cake tin for up to 2 days. Freeze, filled, in a bag or box, for up to a month.

- If using paper cases, don't overfill or the mixture will not rise evenly and get to the tin sides – leave a gap at the top of each case

- Be sure to buy real lemon curd – check that the ingredients contain eggs, butter and lemons, and no preservative

- To ring the changes, if you like, use orange curd or apricot jam

100 g (4 oz) butter
100 g (4 oz) caster sugar
100 g (4 oz) self-raising flour
1 tsp baking powder
2 eggs
6 tsp luxury lemon curd
icing sugar, for dusting

Preheat oven to 180°C/fan160°C/gas 4. Grease (or line with paper cases) a 12-hole bun tin. Put all the ingredients except the lemon curd into a bowl and beat with a wooden spoon until combined and smooth. Divide among the bun holes or paper cases with a spoon. Bake in the preheated oven for about 15 mins until well risen and golden brown; in the Aga, use the grid shelf on the floor of the roasting oven with the cold sheet on the second set of runners for 12 mins. Set aside to cool. Once cold, cut out a shallow cone shape vertically from the centre of each cake. Fill each hole with ½ teaspoon lemon curd and replace each cone at a slight angle on top of the lemon curd. Dust with icing sugar to serve.

## Fun Gingerbread Family

These are a tiny bit tricky, so you'll need to be quite hands on, but they're worth it as they're essentially enchanting for kids – cue the cutting out then the decoration, for which invention and creativity is all. Makes about 10 biscuits. Store in a box in the fridge for up to 2 days. Freezes well in a box for up to a month.

- Don't add too much egg or get the dough too sticky or it will be difficult to transfer the gingerbread biscuits to the baking sheet. If you add too much liquid, knead in a little more flour until it is the consistency of a pastry dough

- I find it best to roll a quarter of the dough at a time as it is easier to handle and doesn't get too sticky. You can re-roll the dough as much as you need to

- You can buy gingerbread men and women cutters from kitchen shops. Cookie cutters come in all shapes and sizes, so you could make other shapes too, especially at Christmas time when you can make trees, stars and angels

*kids' cakes*

- If you prefer, rather than adding decoration before baking, you can bake the biscuits plain and ice to decorate once completely cold

175 g (6 oz) plain flour
½ tsp bicarbonate of soda
75 g (3 oz) light muscovado sugar
2 tsp ground ginger
50 g (2 oz) butter, plus extra for greasing
2 tbsp golden sugar
½ egg, beaten
*for decorating*
a selection of currants or raisins or Smarties, snipped dried apricots, cranberries, liquorice or nuts, as you wish

Preheat oven to 190°C/fan170°C/gas 5. Grease two baking sheets with butter. Put the flour, bicarbonate of soda, sugar and ginger into a bowl. Using fingers, rub in the butter until the mixture resembles fine bread-crumbs. Stir in the golden syrup and egg, mixing with a wooden spoon to a smooth dough. Roll out the dough on a floured worktop to about

5 mm (¼ in). Cut out the gingerbread men with the cutter and arrange on the prepared baking sheets. Use the fruit or suggested alternatives for the eyes, mouth and buttons. Bake in the preheated oven until dark golden for about 12 mins; in the Aga, on the grid shelf on the floor of the roasting oven with the cold sheet on the second set of runners for 8–10 mins. Cool a little in the tin then, using a fish slice, lift carefully on to a wire rack to cool completely.

## Sultana Drop Scones

Traditionally made on a solid metal griddle pan over an open fire, these days drop scones are more easily made in a non-stick frying pan. Their simplicity makes them perfect for children to make with supervision. Makes about 24 scones. Store in a box or plastic bag in the fridge for up to 2 days but best made and eaten fresh. Freeze in a bag for up to a month.

- Made with a batter, not a dough, so sometimes known as Scotch pancakes

- For best results, the batter should be the dropping consistency of double cream

- Use your largest heavy-based non-stick frying pan; Aga users can cook directly on the greased simmering plate (don't leave the lid up on the simmering plate too long or the Aga will lose a lot of heat)

- If using a frying pan, preheat and lightly oil it before cooking the first batch of scones

- As a variation, replace the sultanas with the same amount of snipped dried apricots or grated cooking apple mixed into the batter. You can add a touch of ground cinnamon or mixed spice to the batter too

- Nice to serve warm – so eat as soon as made or put in the toaster or under the grill to reheat

- Good for breakfast with maple syrup; for savoury breakfast, replace the sultanas and maple syrup with snipped fresh chives, salt and pepper, and serve with crispy bacon and fried egg

175 g (6 oz) self-raising flour
1 tsp baking powder
40 g (1½ oz) caster sugar
1 egg
about 200 ml (7 fl oz) milk
50 g (2 oz) sultanas
a little oil, for brushing

*kids' cakes*

Put the flour, baking powder and sugar in a mixing bowl. Make a well in the centre then add the egg and half the milk. Whisk well until smooth and thick then beat in enough of the remaining milk to make the batter the consistency of double cream. Add the sultanas to the batter. Heat a non-stick frying pan over a high heat and brush lightly with oil; for the Aga, lift the lid on the simmering plate for about 3 mins to cool down a little then pour a little oil on to kitchen paper and rub on to the simmering plate. Drop the mixture in dessertspoonfuls directly on to the pan or simmering plate, spacing them well apart to allow for spreading (you'll need to make them in batches). When bubbles appear on the surface, flip the scones with a palette knife and cook on the other side for a further 30 secs–1 min until they are golden brown. Lift the scones on to a wire rack and cover with a clean tea towel to keep them soft. Repeat with the remaining mixture. Serve at once with butter and golden or maple syrup, or honey or jam.

# ask lucy

I have been a professional baker for two decades, during which time I have had my baking triumphs and flops, just like everyone else. Over the years the same issues tend to crop up again and again. Here is a selection of the questions I am most frequently asked, which may help you to understand how to put things right when they go wrong – and how to make sure they don't go wrong in the first place.

*Q. Will adding more baking powder make my cakes more likely to rise?*
*A.* Don't be tempted to add a little extra in the belief that it will help your cake to rise – it will initially, in the oven, but will then collapse while cooling, leaving that telltale central dip. Always follow the recipe and weigh baking powder accurately – preferably with a measuring spoon.

*Q. If I only have spread in my fridge, is it OK to use it instead of butter?*
*A.* You do need to use special baking fat: look on the back of the tub

for a high fat content, over 70 per cent fat is classed as a margarine, but some tubs are as low as 35 per cent; to make a successful cake you need over 59 per cent – this is the key to success. Otherwise, your cake is likely to turn out flat, as spreads have more water than margarine or butter.

*Q. What's the difference between an extract and an essence?*
*A.* Extract is a pure concentrate, a flavouring derived from the actual ingredient; essence is essentially a fake or synthetic, manufactured product. For authenticity and taste, I prefer almond extract, which is taken from the nut. The same applies to vanilla extract, taken from the vanilla plant, and my advice would be to use this; not the manufactured vanilla essence.

*Q. What's behind the advice not to over-beat a cake mix?*
*A.* Over-beating causes a cake to lose volume (even for an all-in-one cake) and make it less likely to rise; you will end up with a dense cake. When making a cake in a food processor, take particular care not to over-whiz. But even when hand-mixing, muffins, for example, prefer a light touch.

*Q. Is it important to use the tin size and shape specified in the recipe?*
*A.* Yes, it's vital; otherwise this will alter the cooking time – more or less, depending on whether you went larger or smaller. Your cake will end up either over-cooked and dry with a tough outer crust or soggily under-cooked.

*Q. If the recipe specifies a 23-cm square cake tin can I use a 23-cm round tin instead?*
*A.* There is a general rule that you should use one size smaller for a square tin; so, for example, if the recipe specifies a 23 cm square tin you would use a 25 cm round one.

*Q. How can I be sure my cake is cooked?*
*A.* This rather depends on the cake. For example, a light sponge cake should be well risen, golden brown and shrinking from the sides of the tin. Press the centre of the cake with your finger – if the sponge springs back, the cake is cooked; if the fingerprint indent remains, it needs to go back in the oven for a bit.

For a denser cake, such as a fruit cake, use a skewer to pierce the centre; if it comes out clean, the cake is cooked. Biscuits are cooked when they are slightly darker round the edge, and the centre is soft but not oily. They become crisper as they cool.

*Q. Why does the top of my cake sometimes crack or peak?*
A. Your oven may be too hot – the cake will rise too quickly due to the high temperature and form a crust, which then cracks. This also happens if the cake is too high in the oven.

*Q. Why do my cakes sink in the middle?*
A. You may have added too much baking powder, so the cake rises too much and then falls. Or, perhaps, you opened the oven door too soon – leave at least 15 mins, or halfway through baking for cakes with short cooking times, before checking then shut the door carefully because a gush of air will shock the cake and prevent rising. Or, it may be that, if it's a sponge, it is under-cooked – under-cooked sponges sink in the middle.

*Q. Sometimes my cakes just don't rise and come out heavy and compact.*
A. It's most likely one of the two following options: either too much

liquid in the cake mix; you need to weigh milk accurately or the cake will be heavy and flat. Or, it could be that your oven is too cool and the raising agents have not had the chance to react.

*Q. Why does the fruit sink to the bottom of a fruit or cherry cake?*
*A.* This only happens if the cake mix is too soft, contains too much liquid or is over-beaten. Alternatively, fruit sinks if it is too wet or syrupy – which is why, for example, when using glacé cherries, it is important to wash off the syrup and dry the cherries well. A cake, such as a Christmas cake, should be fine whatever you do, as it is packed with fruit; the more fruit in a cake, the harder it is for the fruit to sink.

*Q. Recently I baked a cake that was undercooked but burnt at the base.*
*A.* This is a tricky one, as modern ovens have many different settings, so it depends on the oven. However, for successful cakes I suggest using the fan setting, in which the air circulates around the oven. Never bake a cake on the base of the oven: even in a fan oven this is the hottest part. Always bake a cake on an oven shelf that has struts for the air to circulate evenly around the tin. In an Aga the most usual place to bake

a sponge is on the grid shelf on the floor of the baking oven, with the cold sheet on the second set of runners.

Q. *How do I get my hot cake out of a loose-bottomed tin?*
A. When the cake comes out of the oven, run a small palette knife around the edge of the tin and leave the cake in the tin to cool for a few minutes. Then sit the cake on a tall jar or tin and using a tea towel carefully push the sides down to release the cake. Remove the base and carefully transfer to a cooling rack to cool completely.

Q. *Can't I just turn out my cake on to a plate rather than a wire cooling rack?*
A. The point of a wire rack is to make sure that air gets to the base of the cake as it cools – if you put a hot cake on a plate or any dense, flat surface straight from the oven or tin, the air will not be able to reach the base, so any moisture will be trapped there as it cools and the cake will end up soggy at the base. To avoid a cake rack mark on your cake, cover the rack with a clean tea towel before inverting the cake. Once turned out, turn back over, remove tea towel and put back on to the rack to cool completely.

*Q. Jam or cream first in scones?*

A. The jury's still out: in the West Country, for example, there are different rules depending on whether you are in Cornwall or Devon. Personally, I prefer to put the jam on first and then top with a dollop of cream – and there's no need to butter scones if you're using cream.

*Q. What about special diets? My husband has high cholesterol – so how can he enjoy cakes at family teas?*

A. You can make cakes with no eggs, cakes without dairy, sugar-free cakes and low- or no-fat cakes, depending on your requirements. Egg-free cakes are ideal if you have to watch your cholesterol; as are some fatless sponges, based on Swiss roll recipes; use low-fat yogurt instead of cream or jam in fillings to keep down the fat content. Remember that a cake without fat is better eaten fresh (fat acts as a preservative) and will not keep for more than 2 days in the fridge.

# thank yous

A big, big thank you to Helen Armitage, who has edited this book, and been a pleasure to work with and a true professional to the finest detail. Thank you, too, to Vicky Orchard at Ebury Press for masterminding the project – the jacket couldn't be cuter!

*This book is for all my nieces, nephews and godchildren, whom I hope will use it for years to come and enjoy baking now and when they are older! For Hannah, Gabriella, Oliver, Amber, Dominic, Louis, Jacob, Isabella, Polly, Harry, Christian, Purdey, Louis B, Isabel and Annabelle.*

# Conversion charts

Apart from the usual basic measures, such as teaspoon, tablespoon and pinch, all the quantities and measurements in this book are given in both metric and imperial. Spoon measurements are level unless otherwise specified.

## Spoon Measures

Due to the nature of most of the recipes in this book, differences in tablespoon capacity should not have any adverse effect on the taste of the food.

- 1 teaspoon = 5ml
- 1 British tablespoon = 15ml
- 1 American tablespoon = 14.2ml
- 1 Australian tablespoon = 20ml

## Cup Measures

US/AUS cup = 250ml (8 fl oz)

## Approximate Liquid Conversions

| British | USA/AUS |
| --- | --- |
| 4 tablespoons | $1/4$ cup |
| 125ml (4fl oz) | $1/2$ cup |
| 250 ml (8fl oz) | 1 cup |
| 10fl oz/1/2 pint | $1^{1}/4$ cups |
| 450ml (3/4 pint) | 2 cups |
| 600ml (1 pint) | $2^{1}/2$ cups |

## Approximate Solid Conversions

| British | USA/AUS |
| --- | --- |
| 500g (1lb) butter | 2 cups |
| 200g (7Ooz) long grain rice | 1 cup |
| 500g (1 lb) sugar | 2 cups |
| 50g (2oz) chopped onion | $1/2$ cup |
| 50g (2oz) soft breadcrumbs | 1 cup |
| 125g (40z) dry breadcrumbs | 1 cup |
| 500g (1lb) plain flour | 4 cups |
| 50g (2oz) thinly sliced mushrooms | $1/2$ cup |
| 125g (4oz) grated Cheddar (lightly packed) | 1 cup |
| 125g (4 oz) chopped nuts | 1 cup |

# Specialist equipment & suppliers

For additional information, visit my website www.lucyoung.co.uk.

*For kitchenware*
Lakeland Ltd
Tel: 015394 88100 (24 hours)
Fax: 015394 88300
www.lakeland.co.uk

*For catering-equipment supplies*
Nisbets plc
Tel: 0845 140 5555
Fax: 0845 143 5555 (24 hours)
E-mail: sales@nisbets.co.uk or custserv@nisbets.co.uk
www.nisbets.co.uk

*For appliances, ovens etc.*
KitchenAid
Customer services: 0800 988 1566
Tel: +44 (0)208 616 5148
www.kitchenaid.co.uk

Magimix UK Ltd
Tel: +44 (0)1483 427411
Fax: +44 (0)1483 427414
E-mail: enquiries@magimixuk.co.uk
www.magimix.com

Aga
Head Office: 0845 8152020
Sales: 0845 7125207
Technical helpline: 0845 2638178
Customer services: Tel: 0845 6023015
www.aga-web.co.uk

*specialist equipment & suppliers*